JUMBLE®
Garden

It's the
Season to
Pluck These
Plentiful
Puzzles!

Henri Arnold
and
Bob Lee

Jumble® is a registered trademark
of Tribune Media Services, Inc.
Copyright © 2019 by Tribune Media Services, Inc.
All rights reserved.
This book is available in quantity at special discounts
for your group or organization.

For further information, contact:
Triumph Books LLC
814 North Franklin Street
Chicago, Illinois 60610
Phone: (312) 337-0747
www.triumphbooks.com

Printed in U.S.A.
ISBN: 978-1-629-37653-0

Design by Sue Knopf

Contents

JUMBLE®
Garden

Classic
Puzzles

JUMBLE®

Unscramble these four Jumbles, one letter
to each square, to form four ordinary words.

CAZER

DIEFT

MINUME

YUGLIT

GOOD NUTRITION

COULD BE AN EXPERT
WEIGHT LIFTER —
OR DROPPER.

Now arrange the circled letters to form
the surprise answer, as suggested by the
above cartoon.

Print answer here **A**

JUMBLE®

Unscramble these four Jumbles, one letter to each square, to form four ordinary words.

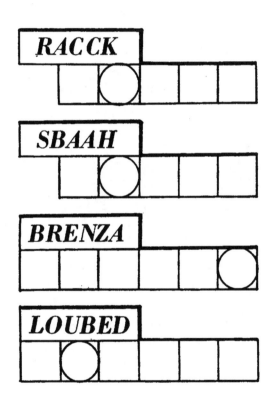

RACCK

SBAAH

BRENZA

LOUBED

Boss, I'm tired of being pushed around!

You're fired!

WHAT YOU WERE THE DAY YOU FIRST MADE YOURSELF HEARD.

Now arrange the circled letters to form the surprise answer, as suggested by the above cartoon.

Print answer here ◯◯◯◯

3

JUMBLE®

Unscramble these four Jumbles, one letter to each square, to form four ordinary words.

Kill the author!

ON ACCOUNT OF THIS THE DRAMATIST WAS AFRAID FOR HIS LIFE!

WOGAL

UMPEL

LAISEY

MYFAIL

Now arrange the circled letters to form the surprise answer, as suggested by the above cartoon.

Print answer here " ⬡⬡⬡⬡ ⬡⬡⬡⬡ "

JUMBLE®

Unscramble these four Jumbles, one letter
to each square, to form four ordinary words.

YIRAH

WOGIN

CHETOL

GARNAL

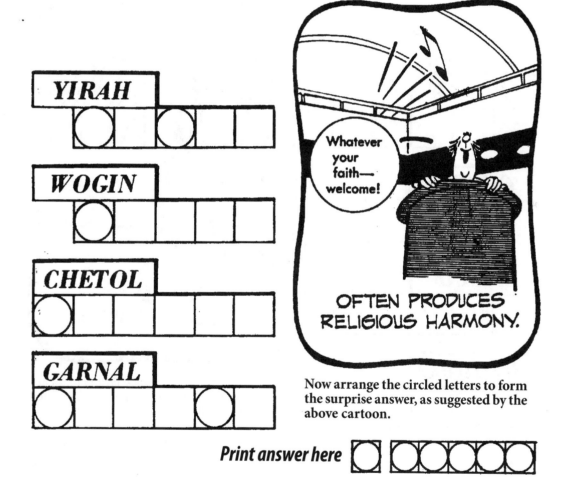

Whatever your faith— welcome!

OFTEN PRODUCES
RELIGIOUS HARMONY.

Now arrange the circled letters to form
the surprise answer, as suggested by the
above cartoon.

Print answer here

JUMBLE®

Unscramble these four Jumbles, one letter
to each square, to form four ordinary words.

OCHAM

CHABT

HISMAF

ROHRRO

VISIT
ENGLAND

TRAVEL
AGENCY

USED TO
"RULE THE WAVES."

Now arrange the circled letters to form
the surprise answer, as suggested by the
above cartoon.

Print answer here

6

JUMBLE®

Unscramble these four Jumbles, one letter
to each square, to form four ordinary words.

HEYNO

GOGER

REFTER

MYDIAS

The waist seems to fit perfectly

Okay

THE GIRTH COULD BE CORRECT.

Now arrange the circled letters to form
the surprise answer, as suggested by the
above cartoon.

Print answer here " ◯◯◯◯◯ "

7

JUMBLE®

Unscramble these four Jumbles, one letter
to each square, to form four ordinary words.

YERME

TANCH

ROOMAN

ABHORR

WHAT TIME
AND GRIME DO.

Now arrange the circled letters to form
the surprise answer, as suggested by the
above cartoon.

Print answer here

JUMBLE®

Unscramble these four Jumbles, one letter to each square, to form four ordinary words.

NOVEY

DEPIT

INKANP

CLAGEN

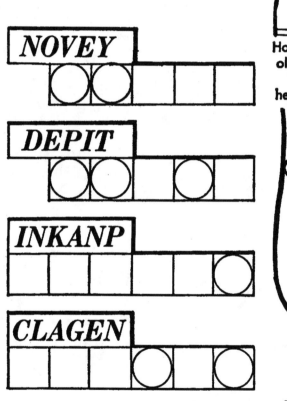

How old is he?

A teenager

WITH THIS ONE'S REQUIRED TO MAKE A SCORE.

Now arrange the circled letters to form the surprise answer, as suggested by the above cartoon.

Print answer here

9

JUMBLE®

Unscramble these four Jumbles, one letter
to each square, to form four ordinary words.

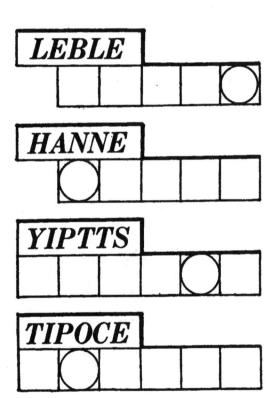

LEBLE

HANNE

YIPTTS

TIPOCE

They never
make up
their mind!

WHAT A CHANGE
OF SHOE SHOWS.

Now arrange the circled letters to form
the surprise answer, as suggested by the
above cartoon.

Print answer here

10

JUMBLE®

Unscramble these four Jumbles, one letter
to each square, to form four ordinary words.

SINOE

CAMPH

MERUDE

NEEVEL

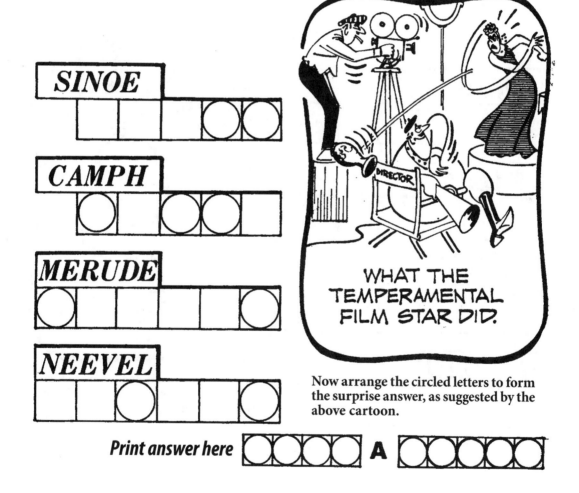

WHAT THE
TEMPERAMENTAL
FILM STAR DID.

Now arrange the circled letters to form
the surprise answer, as suggested by the
above cartoon.

Print answer here ☐☐☐☐☐ A ☐☐☐☐☐☐

11

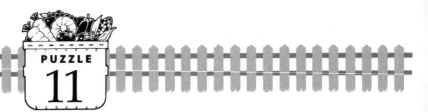

JUMBLE®

Unscramble these four Jumbles, one letter
to each square, to form four ordinary words.

DURIL

VALEG

CATNIG

GAPOAD

CITY
LIGHTING
CO.

THIS HORSE
APPEARS TO HAVE
SOME CONNECTION
WITH ELECTRICITY.

Now arrange the circled letters to form
the surprise answer, as suggested by the
above cartoon.

Print answer here ⬡ ⬡⬡⬡⬡

JUMBLE®

Unscramble these four Jumbles, one letter to each square, to form four ordinary words.

ENCAP
○ ○ ☐ ☐ ○

RUTTE
○ ☐ ☐ ○ ☐

EVITLY
○ ○ ☐ ☐ ☐ ☐

TEGOTH
○ ○ ☐ ☐ ○ ☐

One more and I'll pass out!

ONCE TAKEN YOU'RE BOUND TO GO UNDER.

Now arrange the circled letters to form the surprise answer, as suggested by the above cartoon.

Print answer here ○○○ ○○○○○○

JUMBLE®

Unscramble these four Jumbles, one letter
to each square, to form four ordinary words.

KEVAN

LYDAM

SHATAM

CEERUD

WHAT HE WAS
AFTER LEAVING
THE TATTOO PARLOR.

Now arrange the circled letters to form
the surprise answer, as suggested by the
above cartoon.

Print answer here **A**

JUMBLE®

Unscramble these four Jumbles, one letter
to each square, to form four ordinary words.

URROF

CAUMS

PRIMEE

FANNIT

This is how we
concealed the evidence

PROVIDE THE
LISTENERS WITH
A COVER-UP.

Now arrange the circled letters to form
the surprise answer, as suggested by the
above cartoon.

Print answer here

JUMBLE®

Unscramble these four Jumbles, one letter to each square, to form four ordinary words.

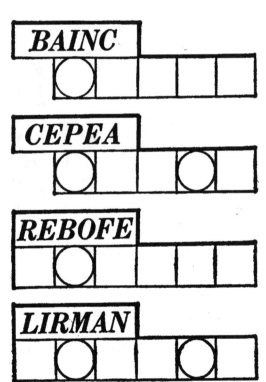

BAINC

CEPEA

REBOFE

LIRMAN

SOUNDS LIKE HEADGEAR FOR A POLAR EXPLORER.

Now arrange the circled letters to form the surprise answer, as suggested by the above cartoon.

Print answer here **AN**

JUMBLE®

Unscramble these four Jumbles, one letter
to each square, to form four ordinary words.

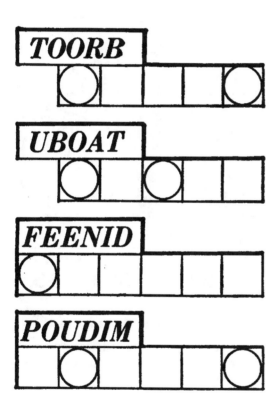

TOORB

UBOAT

FEENID

POUDIM

Finished?

IF YOU USE IT,
YOUR ENTRANCE
WON'T LEAVE A
BAD IMPRESSION.

Now arrange the circled letters to form
the surprise answer, as suggested by the
above cartoon.

Print answer here A

JUMBLE®

Unscramble these four Jumbles, one letter to each square, to form four ordinary words.

ATEAB

RODIF

AFAIRS

DROWPE

TEASES WITH BONES.

Now arrange the circled letters to form the surprise answer, as suggested by the above cartoon.

Print answer here

18

JUMBLE®

Unscramble these four Jumbles, one letter to each square, to form four ordinary words.

DISTA
◯ ◯ □ □ ◯

TEELA
□ □ ◯ □

GINKAB
◯ □ □ □ □ □

ENGOUT
□ □ □ □ ◯

They got out today

Glad I got my dough back!

WHEN DISCHARGED THEY DISAPPEAR.

Now arrange the circled letters to form the surprise answer, as suggested by the above cartoon.

Print answer here ◯ ◯ ◯ ◯ ◯

JUMBLE®

Unscramble these four Jumbles, one letter
to each square, to form four ordinary words.

SUHOE

TAUDI

BLYMAC

CERAPH

SOUNDS AS THOUGH
YOU'RE BEING PURSUED
WHEN YOU'RE JUST
BEING MODEST.

Now arrange the circled letters to form
the surprise answer, as suggested by the
above cartoon.

Print answer here

JUMBLE®

Unscramble these four Jumbles, one letter
to each square, to form four ordinary words.

MAWPS

NATEC

YENICT

SHEERA

Someone you know?

(GULP)
My b-boss!

A NODDING ACQUAINTANCE.

Now arrange the circled letters to form
the surprise answer, as suggested by the
above cartoon.

Print answer here

21

JUMBLE®

Unscramble these four Jumbles, one letter
to each square, to form four ordinary words.

FENTO

ZIERP

ROTHEY

CAULNY

I'm splitting!

But you've only
done half!

T'S GROUP

ONLY ONE SIDE
WAS RECORDED
BY THE ARTIST.

Now arrange the circled letters to form
the surprise answer, as suggested by the
above cartoon.

Print answer here **A**

22

JUMBLE®

Unscramble these four Jumbles, one letter
to each square, to form four ordinary words.

CHUGO

REEMB

HUMBAS

DITNIC

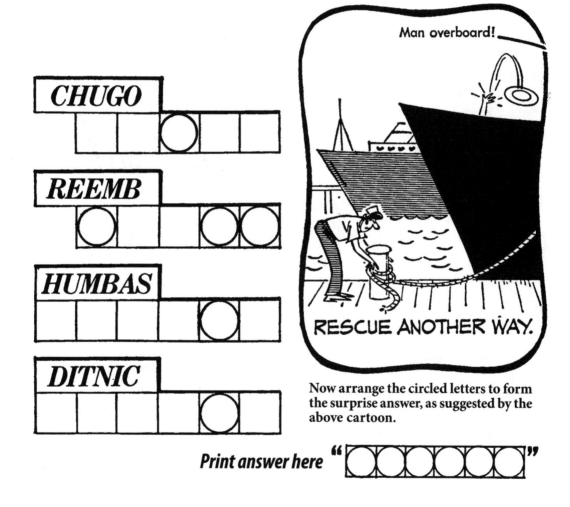

Man overboard!

RESCUE ANOTHER WAY.

Now arrange the circled letters to form
the surprise answer, as suggested by the
above cartoon.

Print answer here " ⃝⃝⃝⃝⃝⃝ "

23

JUMBLE®

Unscramble these four Jumbles, one letter to each square, to form four ordinary words.

AYLIG

FIRRA

CLINEP

NERCRO

HOW A BREADWINNER IS NOT APT TO SPEND HIS TIME.

Now arrange the circled letters to form the surprise answer, as suggested by the above cartoon.

Print answer here

JUMBLE®

Unscramble these four Jumbles, one letter
to each square, to form four ordinary words.

GIRRO

POAZT

TACTIN

URAUBE

He got
the
answer
in a
second!

He can't
be human!

72,683½ √1,073,272,321

ONE IS SUPPOSED TO
THINK MECHANICALLY.

Now arrange the circled letters to form
the surprise answer, as suggested by the
above cartoon.

Print answer here

JUMBLE®

Unscramble these four Jumbles, one letter to each square, to form four ordinary words.

ADDIE

YOMEN

DIRNEH

GOYAVE

Marrying beneath her

THE GOOD NAME SHE LOST WHEN SHE GOT MARRIED.

Now arrange the circled letters to form the surprise answer, as suggested by the above cartoon.

Print answer here " ◯◯◯◯◯◯ "

JUMBLE®
Garden

Daily
Puzzles

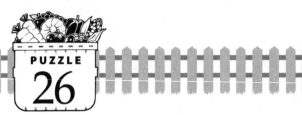

JUMBLE®

Unscramble these four Jumbles, one letter
to each square, to form four ordinary words.

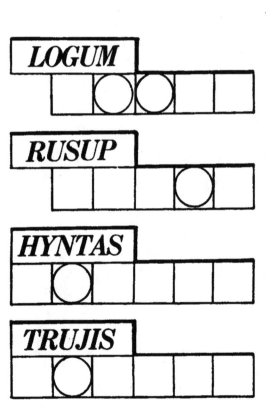

LOGUM

RUSUP

HYNTAS

TRUJIS

IT MAY BE THIS ON
A GOLFER WHEN
HE'S IN IT.

Now arrange the circled letters to form
the surprise answer, as suggested by the
above cartoon.

Print answer here "⬡⬡⬡⬡⬡"

JUMBLE®

Unscramble these four Jumbles, one letter
to each square, to form four ordinary words.

WAMAC

SNAPY

NELPOY

URRUMM

You'll go far

INCLINED TO RISE TO
A HIGHER LEVEL.

Now arrange the circled letters to form
the surprise answer, as suggested by the
above cartoon.

Print answer here

JUMBLE

Unscramble these four Jumbles, one letter
to each square, to form four ordinary words.

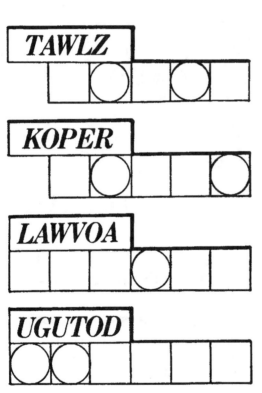

TAWLZ

KOPER

LAWVOA

UGUTOD

CURED PATIENTS

You're all OK

AFTER TREATMENT,
HOSPITAL PATIENTS
ARE EXPECTED TO GO
TOWARD THIS WARD.

Now arrange the circled letters to form
the surprise answer, as suggested by the
above cartoon.

Print answer here " ◯◯◯◯◯◯◯ "

JUMBLE®

Unscramble these four Jumbles, one letter
to each square, to form four ordinary words.

NUKKS

BOYTO

INBELB

TIDSEW

HEADED FOR
WINTER SPORTS.

Now arrange the circled letters to form
the surprise answer, as suggested by the
above cartoon.

Print answer here " ⬡⬡⬡⬡ ⬡⬡⬡⬡⬡ "

JUMBLE

Unscramble these four Jumbles, one letter
to each square, to form four ordinary words.

RYKUM

DEPTY

NIRFIM

BLIGET

They won't
dare punish
ALL of us!

HOW LITTLE DEVILS
GET TOGETHER.

Now arrange the circled letters to form
the surprise answer, as suggested by the
above cartoon.

Print answer here **WITH** " ☐☐☐ — ☐☐☐☐☐ "

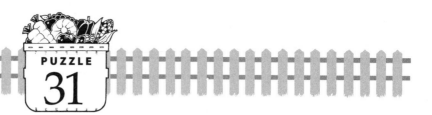

JUMBLE®

Unscramble these four Jumbles, one letter
to each square, to form four ordinary words.

GALEE

SYRTT

UNBREM

PHOUST

WHAT SHE SAID
WHEN THE SCULPTOR
ARRIVED.

Now arrange the circled letters to form
the surprise answer, as suggested by the
above cartoon.

Print answer here "◯◯◯ – ◯◯◯?"

JUMBLE®

Unscramble these four Jumbles, one letter to each square, to form four ordinary words.

DITIO

RATAO

FLANEL

LEARNY

It is NOT spoiled!

Now arrange the circled letters to form the surprise answer, as suggested by the above cartoon.

Print answer here " ◯◯◯◯◯ "

JUMBLE®

Unscramble these four Jumbles, one letter
to each square, to form four ordinary words.

RIMPE

USSOE

PANICT

HARMIO

Missed
my
plane!

Didn't expect
to see HIM back!

REGISTERED
UNEXPECTEDLY.

Now arrange the circled letters to form
the surprise answer, as suggested by the
above cartoon.

Print answer here

JUMBLE®

Unscramble these four Jumbles, one letter
to each square, to form four ordinary words.

WOSOP

STUQE

DYRAMI

AEDING

Get it?
HA HA
R?

WHY A JOKE CAUSED
THE CARPENTER
TO HURT HIS THUMB.

Now arrange the circled letters to form
the surprise answer, as suggested by the
above cartoon.

*Print
answer
here*   HE ⬡⬡⬡⬡⬡⬡ THE ⬡⬡⬡⬡⬡

JUMBLE®

Unscramble these four Jumbles, one letter
to each square, to form four ordinary words.

You're
getting
his
job

THE ACME CO.

PRES.

A RESPECTFUL
POSITION ON
THE STAFF.

MASCK

FLOTY

WHOSAD

ASHRIP

Now arrange the circled letters to form
the surprise answer, as suggested by the
above cartoon.

Print answer here ◯◯◯◯ – ◯◯◯◯

JUMBLE

Unscramble these four Jumbles, one letter
to each square, to form four ordinary words.

CHARP

LADLY

RESPON

ENGAVE

That'll improve your score

PRO SHOP

A CONVENIENT HAT FOR GOLF.

Now arrange the circled letters to form
the surprise answer, as suggested by the
above cartoon.

Print answer here A " ⬡⬡⬡⬡⬡⬡ ⬡⬡⬡ "

JUMBLE®

Unscramble these four Jumbles, one letter
to each square, to form four ordinary words.

TELIT

RYHUR

HYSERR

THORCC

Come here—and
beat that girl!

Now arrange the circled letters to form
the surprise answer, as suggested by the
above cartoon.

Print answer here " ◯◯◯ - ◯◯◯ "

JUMBLE®

Unscramble these four Jumbles, one letter
to each square, to form four ordinary words.

THOAL

KETOS

YENKOD

HAWLIE

JOE'S BAR

WHAT YOU MIGHT
SEE AT A BAR ON
A RAINY NIGHT.

Now arrange the circled letters to form
the surprise answer, as suggested by the
above cartoon.

Print answer here **AN** ☐☐☐ ☐☐☐☐

JUMBLE®

Unscramble these four Jumbles, one letter
to each square, to form four ordinary words.

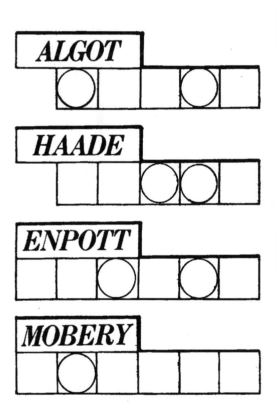

ALGOT

HAADE

ENPOTT

MOBERY

Handsome
and rich!

THIS WEALTHY MAN
SOUNDS "ATTRACTIVE."

Now arrange the circled letters to form
the surprise answer, as suggested by the
above cartoon.

Print answer here A

41

JUMBLE®

Unscramble these four Jumbles, one letter
to each square, to form four ordinary words.

COLIG

KNEAT

ROBUGE

TRYAGE

I'm cuttin' in!

Oh, yeah?

TWO TO ONE IT CAUSES TROUBLE!

Now arrange the circled letters to form
the surprise answer, as suggested by the
above cartoon.

Print answer here **A**

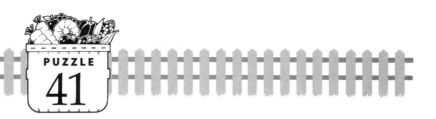

JUMBLE®

Unscramble these four Jumbles, one letter to each square, to form four ordinary words.

VANER

HEALT

REFOLG

LARPIL

See how much bigger it makes the room look!

GENERAL REARRANGEMENT— WITH GREATER SCOPE.

Now arrange the circled letters to form the surprise answer, as suggested by the above cartoon.

Print answer here

43

JUMBLE®

Unscramble these four Jumbles, one letter
to each square, to form four ordinary words.

TAPAD

EVVAL

LIPPUT

YALMES

USEFUL IF YOU GO
IN FOR SPOONING
IN A BIG WAY!

Now arrange the circled letters to form
the surprise answer, as suggested by the
above cartoon.

Print answer here

44

JUMBLE®

Unscramble these four Jumbles, one letter
to each square, to form four ordinary words.

SINBO

EMZIA

JOADIN

LEMETH

Women make ME SAD

Now arrange the circled letters to form
the surprise answer, as suggested by the
above cartoon.

Print answer here "⬜⬜⬜⬜⬜"

JUMBLE®

Unscramble these four Jumbles, one letter to each square, to form four ordinary words.

FLAUW

KUSHY

TARROO

NUTHAG

HOW TO GET RID OF A TIRESOME CUSTOMER.

BOOTS

Now arrange the circled letters to form the surprise answer, as suggested by the above cartoon.

Print answer here ⬡⬡⬡⬡ **HIM** ⬡⬡⬡⬡

46

JUMBLE®

Unscramble these four Jumbles, one letter
to each square, to form four ordinary words.

DREEL

KYACT

TESHEE

AHVEBE

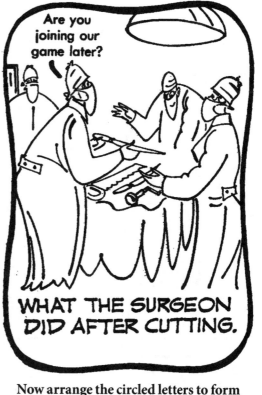

Are you
joining our
game later?

WHAT THE SURGEON
DID AFTER CUTTING.

Now arrange the circled letters to form
the surprise answer, as suggested by the
above cartoon.

Print answer here

JUMBLE®

Unscramble these four Jumbles, one letter
to each square, to form four ordinary words.

GYROL

SEGIN

REYGES

INBOUN

WHAT THE FIRST
LETTER FROM HIS
GIRL LEFT HIM.

Now arrange the circled letters to form
the surprise answer, as suggested by the
above cartoon.

Print answer here

48

JUMBLE®

Unscramble these four Jumbles, one letter
to each square, to form four ordinary words.

ESOLO

YANGO

INKELT

BLATLE

WHAT HIS
"SHORT STORY"
APPEARED TO BE.

Now arrange the circled letters to form
the surprise answer, as suggested by the
above cartoon.

Print answer here **A** ⬡⬡⬡⬡⬡ ⬡⬡⬡

49

JUMBLE®

Unscramble these four Jumbles, one letter
to each square, to form four ordinary words.

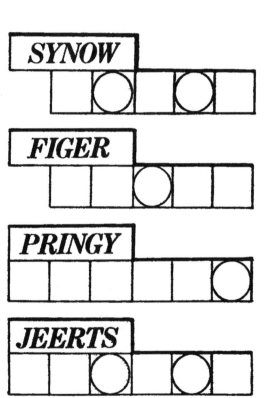

SYNOW

FIGER

PRINGY

JEERTS

Just look
at these!

YOU HAVE TO GIVE
SOME PEOPLE THE
NEEDLE TO
START THIS.

Now arrange the circled letters to form
the surprise answer, as suggested by the
above cartoon.

Print answer here

JUMBLE®

Unscramble these four Jumbles, one letter
to each square, to form four ordinary words.

SCUHR

CEPIE

YOUTCH

RYNFEZ

HE GOT A SLAP ON
THE FACE FOR
MAKING IT.

Now arrange the circled letters to form
the surprise answer, as suggested by the
above cartoon.

Print answer here **A** ◯◯◯◯◯

JUMBLE®

Unscramble these four Jumbles, one letter
to each square, to form four ordinary words.

WIHSS

RADOH

AVEGAS

DINIOE

Is that all?

You know what comes next

IT GENERALLY FOLLOWS
THE LAST COURSE.

Now arrange the circled letters to form
the surprise answer, as suggested by the
above cartoon.

Print answer here

JUMBLE®

Unscramble these four Jumbles, one letter
to each square, to form four ordinary words.

RAALT

NAIRY

SPOMIE

GLERCY

All wrong! Do 'em
over again!

CALL FOR A CHANGE
OF LETTERS.

Now arrange the circled letters to form
the surprise answer, as suggested by the
above cartoon.

Print answer here

JUMBLE®

Unscramble these four Jumbles, one letter
to each square, to form four ordinary words.

RETEX

CANKS

ENVORG

HYGNID

THIS WOMAN'S VOICE
SOUNDS PENETRATING.

Now arrange the circled letters to form
the surprise answer, as suggested by the
above cartoon.

Print answer here **A**

JUMBLE®

Unscramble these four Jumbles, one letter to each square, to form four ordinary words.

DEROO

SUYFS

YURJIN

ROUPAR

WHAT HE BECAME WHEN HE WAS OFFERED I.O.U.'S FOR AN EXPENSIVE COAT.

Now arrange the circled letters to form the surprise answer, as suggested by the above cartoon.

Print answer here "◯◯◯-◯◯◯-◯"

JUMBLE®

Unscramble these four Jumbles, one letter to each square, to form four ordinary words.

PLEEX

ENGAM

DANNIL

LOWLAF

Come down in the autumn!

Who?

Now arrange the circled letters to form the surprise answer, as suggested by the above cartoon.

Print answer here " ⬭⬭⬭⬭ "

JUMBLE®

Unscramble these four Jumbles, one letter to each square, to form four ordinary words.

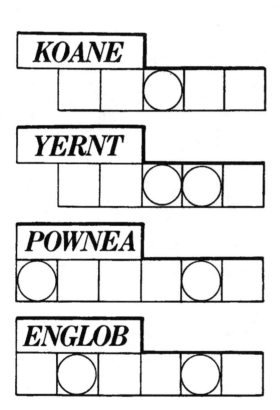

KOANE

YERNT

POWNEA

ENGLOB

BRZT TV SYSTEMS, INC.

THERE ARE MANY OPENINGS IN THIS KIND OF WORK.

Now arrange the circled letters to form the surprise answer, as suggested by the above cartoon.

Print answer here

JUMBLE®

Unscramble these four Jumbles, one letter
to each square, to form four ordinary words.

PRAID
◯◯ ◯◯◯

TISUE
◯◯ ◯◯

HELSUB
◯◯

SICCEN
◯◯ ◯◯◯

THEY DO HOLDUPS
IN PAIRS.

Now arrange the circled letters to form
the surprise answer, as suggested by the
above cartoon.

Print answer here ◯◯◯◯◯◯◯◯◯◯◯◯

JUMBLE®

Unscramble these four Jumbles, one letter
to each square, to form four ordinary words.

ESTED

INAFT

MEHRIT

YULIBS

STARTS EVERY MONTH.

Now arrange the circled letters to form
the surprise answer, as suggested by the
above cartoon.

Print answer here

JUMBLE®

Unscramble these four Jumbles, one letter
to each square, to form four ordinary words.

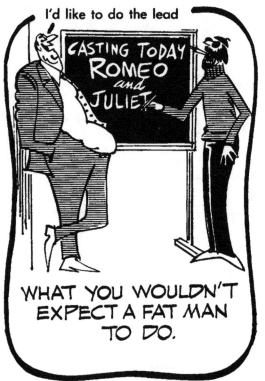

I'd like to do the lead

CASTING TODAY
ROMEO
and
JULIET

WHAT YOU WOULDN'T
EXPECT A FAT MAN
TO DO.

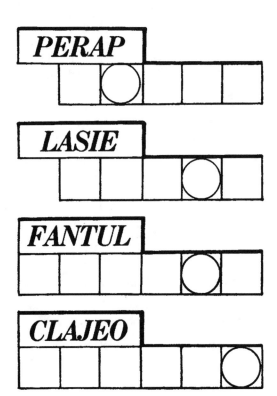

PERAP

LASIE

FANTUL

CLAJEO

Now arrange the circled letters to form
the surprise answer, as suggested by the
above cartoon.

Print answer here " ◯◯◯◯ "

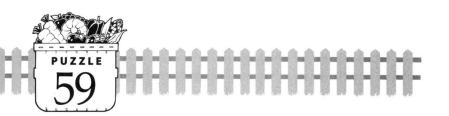

JUMBLE®

Unscramble these four Jumbles, one letter to each square, to form four ordinary words.

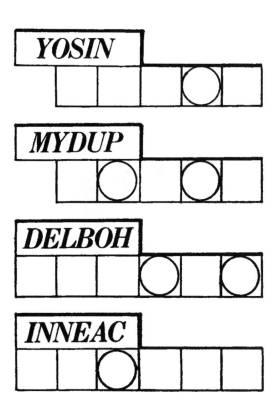

YOSIN

MYDUP

DELBOH

INNEAC

Love to go there for our vacation

Holidays IN BRITAIN

MAY BE SPENT IN ENGLAND?

Now arrange the circled letters to form the surprise answer, as suggested by the above cartoon.

Print answer here

JUMBLE®

Unscramble these four Jumbles, one letter
to each square, to form four ordinary words.

GIMAC

YENEM

MIEPED

FATSIE

I don't get it!

Never says a word

HE ACTS DUMB.

Now arrange the circled letters to form
the surprise answer, as suggested by the
above cartoon.

Print answer here

JUMBLE.

Unscramble these four Jumbles, one letter
to each square, to form four ordinary words.

KNACS

LAROF

LUGGEJ

CEPPIT

WHAT HE WHO
LAUGHS LAST OFTEN
DOESN'T DO.

Now arrange the circled letters to form
the surprise answer, as suggested by the
above cartoon.

Print answer here ◯◯◯ THE ◯◯◯◯

63

JUMBLE®

Unscramble these four Jumbles, one letter
to each square, to form four ordinary words.

NIGVY

GANOW

MELING

STINCH

EXIT

WHAT THE NEAR-
SIGHTED BOXER HAD
TROUBLE FINDING.

Now arrange the circled letters to form
the surprise answer, as suggested by the
above cartoon.

Print answer here THE "◯◯◯◯◯◯ – ◯◯"

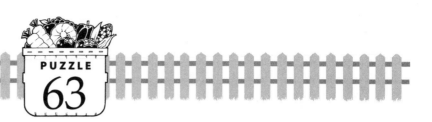

JUMBLE®

Unscramble these four Jumbles, one letter
to each square, to form four ordinary words.

UNHAM

PEROW

LOUBED

SEELAW

WHAT EVE SAID
WHEN ADAM ASKED
WHETHER SHE
STILL LOVED HIM.

Now arrange the circled letters to form
the surprise answer, as suggested by the
above cartoon.

Print answer here ?

JUMBLE®

Unscramble these four Jumbles, one letter
to each square, to form four ordinary words.

THIGE

STYRT

YEUFLE

REGOUM

WHEN IS THE
CHEAPEST TIME TO
PHONE YOUR FRIENDS
BY LONG DISTANCE?

Now arrange the circled letters to form
the surprise answer, as suggested by the
above cartoon.

*Print
answer
here* WHEN ◯◯◯◯◯'◯◯ ◯◯◯

JUMBLE®

Unscramble these four Jumbles, one letter
to each square, to form four ordinary words.

GYROP

RARIF

ROHORR

SEATTE

DID YOU HEAR MY
LAST JOKE?

Now arrange the circled letters to form
the surprise answer, as suggested by the
above cartoon.

Print answer here " ⬡ ⬡⬡⬡⬡ ⬡⬡ "

JUMBLE®

Unscramble these four Jumbles, one letter
to each square, to form four ordinary words.

LAMEY

REBAG

CHERAG

NIPURT

WHAT SOME BEARS
SEEM TO DO IN
WINTERTIME.

Now arrange the circled letters to form
the surprise answer, as suggested by the
above cartoon.

Print answer here " ⬚⬚ - ⬚⬚⬚⬚ - ⬚⬚⬚⬚ "

68

JUMBLE ®

Unscramble these four Jumbles, one letter to each square, to form four ordinary words.

TUMOH

KYACT

GROAND

SMEFLY

THE MAN WHO STOLE A PUDDING WAS TAKEN INTO THIS.

Now arrange the circled letters to form the surprise answer, as suggested by the above cartoon.

Print answer here " ◯◯◯◯◯◯◯◯◯ "

JUMBLE®

Unscramble these four Jumbles, one letter
to each square, to form four ordinary words.

AUPSE

MERFA

NEXETT

TROBEH

I've eaten in
better places

WHAT WAS THE
TROUBLE WITH THE
RESTAURANT THEY
OPENED UP ON
THE MOON?

Now arrange the circled letters to form
the surprise answer, as suggested by the
above cartoon.

Print
answer
here

IT HAD "   "
NO

JUMBLE®

Unscramble these four Jumbles, one letter
to each square, to form four ordinary words.

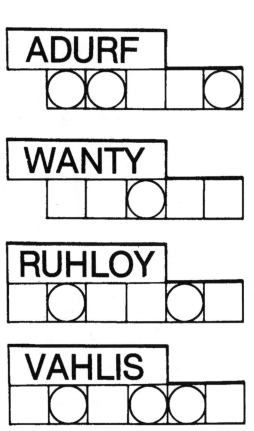

ADURF

WANTY

RUHLOY

VAHLIS

WHAT HE SAID WHEN
TEACHER GAVE HIM
AN "F" ON THE
VOCABULARY TEST.

Now arrange the circled letters to form
the surprise answer, as suggested by the
above cartoon.

*Print answer
here* ⬡⬡⬡⬡⬡ ⬡⬡⬡⬡⬡ ME

JUMBLE®

Unscramble these four Jumbles, one letter to each square, to form four ordinary words.

TURSY

JECET

LAYMIN

SEPPOO

WHERE YOU MIGHT FIND THE SCHOOLMASTER.

Now arrange the circled letters to form the surprise answer, as suggested by the above cartoon.

Print answer here   IN "THE ⬭⬭⬭⬭⬭⬭⬭⬭⬭⬭ "

JUMBLE®

Unscramble these four Jumbles, one letter to each square, to form four ordinary words.

RORYS

HERBT

SULTYS

RUGBBY

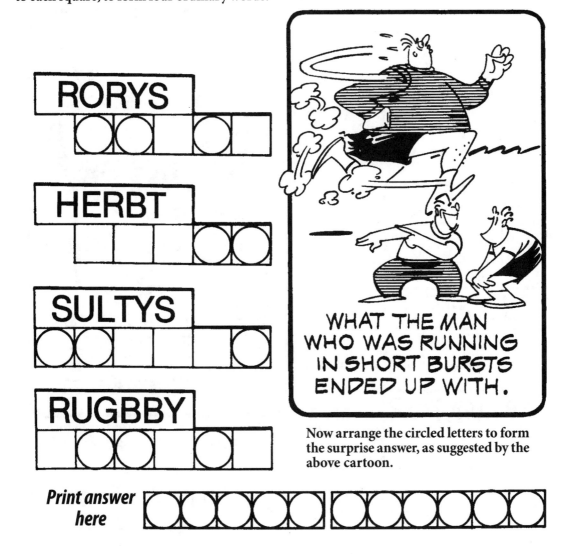

WHAT THE MAN WHO WAS RUNNING IN SHORT BURSTS ENDED UP WITH.

Now arrange the circled letters to form the surprise answer, as suggested by the above cartoon.

Print answer here

73

JUMBLE

Unscramble these four Jumbles, one letter
to each square, to form four ordinary words.

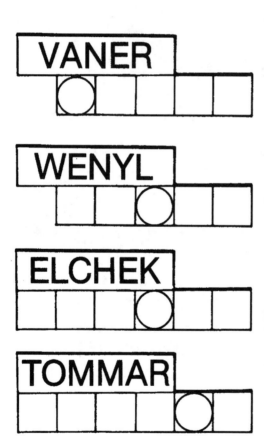

VANER

WENYL

ELCHEK

TOMMAR

I'm shocked!

WHAT FOUR-LETTER
WORD DO SOME
PEOPLE FIND MOST
OBJECTIONABLE?

Now arrange the circled letters to form
the surprise answer, as suggested by the
above cartoon.

Print answer here "  "

74

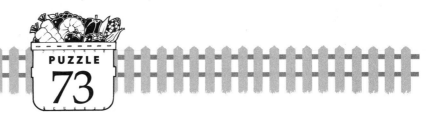

PUZZLE
73

JUMBLE®

Unscramble these four Jumbles, one letter to each square, to form four ordinary words.

IRATT

CURCO

TABBIR

ENWAKE

Another best-seller

WHAT THE SUCCESSFUL NOVELIST MUST HAVE BEEN.

Now arrange the circled letters to form the surprise answer, as suggested by the above cartoon.

Print answer here   ON THE " ◯◯◯◯◯ " ◯◯◯◯◯

75

JUMBLE®

Unscramble these four Jumbles, one letter to each square, to form four ordinary words.

MARAD

FOBEG

DIASUN

GUMMAN

FROM THE SURGEON CAME THESE WORDS.

Now arrange the circled letters to form the surprise answer, as suggested by the above cartoon.

Print answer here "◯◯, ◯◯◯◯◯!"

JUMBLE®

Unscramble these four Jumbles, one letter
to each square, to form four ordinary words.

ROHTT

ILFOO

GIANAU

UMLUTT

Won't he ever forget it?!

THE IMPRESSION MADE
ON ONE WHO'S BEEN
IN THE NAVY MIGHT
BE QUITE LASTING.

Now arrange the circled letters to form
the surprise answer, as suggested by the
above cartoon.

Print answer here

Unscramble these four Jumbles, one letter
to each square, to form four ordinary words.

CENEP

TOCET

NAHZIG

HUCCOR

FISHING MAY BE
A "DISEASE," BUT
IT'S NOT NECES-
SARILY THIS.

Now arrange the circled letters to form
the surprise answer, as suggested by the
above cartoon.

Print answer here " ◯◯◯◯◯◯◯◯◯ "

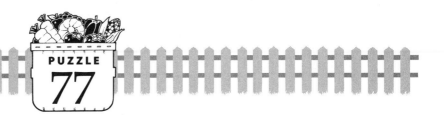

JUMBLE®

Unscramble these four Jumbles, one letter
to each square, to form four ordinary words.

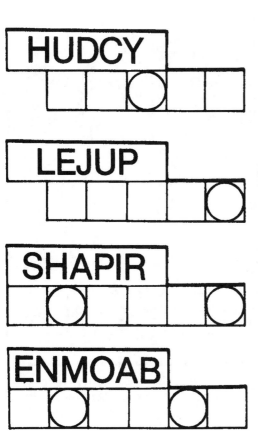

HUDCY

LEJUP

SHAPIR

ENMOAB

DID THEY CALL
HER THIS BECAUSE
SHE HAD A
HEART OF STONE?

Now arrange the circled letters to form
the surprise answer, as suggested by the
above cartoon.

Print answer here

79

JUMBLE®

Unscramble these four Jumbles, one letter
to each square, to form four ordinary words.

UGOBS

KNOTE

LIRMAN

MOANEY

WHAT MUCH SO—
CALLED PRESIDENTIAL
TIMBER OFTEN IS.

Now arrange the circled letters to form
the surprise answer, as suggested by the
above cartoon.

Print answer
here   [ ] [ ] [ ] [ ] [ ] [ ] " [ ] [ ] [ ] [ ] "

JUMBLE®

Unscramble these four Jumbles, one letter
to each square, to form four ordinary words.

LELIS

PAUNC

SUCLEM

SLAQUL

One after another. . .

HOW THAT DON
JUAN TREATED
ALL WOMEN.

Now arrange the circled letters to form
the surprise answer, as suggested by the
above cartoon.

Print answer here " "

81

JUMBLE®

Unscramble these four Jumbles, one letter
to each square, to form four ordinary words.

He's got muscles between
his ears, too

WHERE THE CONCEITED
WEIGHT LIFTER
LET HIS BODY GO.

INSIF

YOHEN

KOHOED

UNTEAB

Now arrange the circled letters to form
the surprise answer, as suggested by the
above cartoon.

Print answer here

JUMBLE®

Unscramble these four Jumbles, one letter
to each square, to form four ordinary words.

GOARC

HAIKK

LOUTTE

TIMOON

WHAT THAT BAKERY
TYCOON WAS.

Now arrange the circled letters to form
the surprise answer, as suggested by the
above cartoon.

Print an-
swer here ONE ☐☐☐☐☐ ☐☐☐☐☐☐

Unscramble these four Jumbles, one letter to each square, to form four ordinary words.

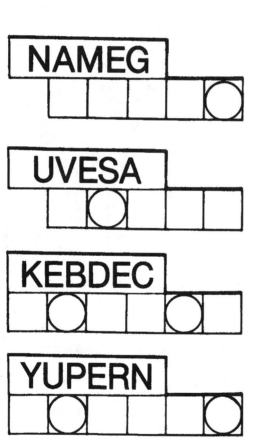

NAMEG

UVESA

KEBDEC

YUPERN

WHAT HER APPEAL SPRANG FROM.

Now arrange the circled letters to form the surprise answer, as suggested by the above cartoon.

Print answer here HER " ☐☐☐ ☐☐☐ "

JUMBLE®

Unscramble these four Jumbles, one letter to each square, to form four ordinary words.

RYDYL

DONSY

NAILET

BELNAG

WHAT HER IDEAL BECAME AFTER SHE MARRIED HIM.

Now arrange the circled letters to form the surprise answer, as suggested by the above cartoon.

Print answer here AN ⬡⬡⬡⬡⬡⬡

JUMBLE®

Unscramble these four Jumbles, one letter
to each square, to form four ordinary words.

ELLAP

RAPOE

INSOUC

CAPTEK

Oh, not again!

WHAT THAT OLD-
TIME GARAGE
MECHANIC WAS
BOTHERED WITH.

Now arrange the circled letters to form
the surprise answer, as suggested by the
above cartoon.

Print answer " ⬡⬡⬡⬡⬡ " ⬡⬡⬡⬡⬡⬡
here

JUMBLE®

Unscramble these four Jumbles, one letter
to each square, to form four ordinary words.

MICER

LUMGO

MOURUQ

SNIBAH

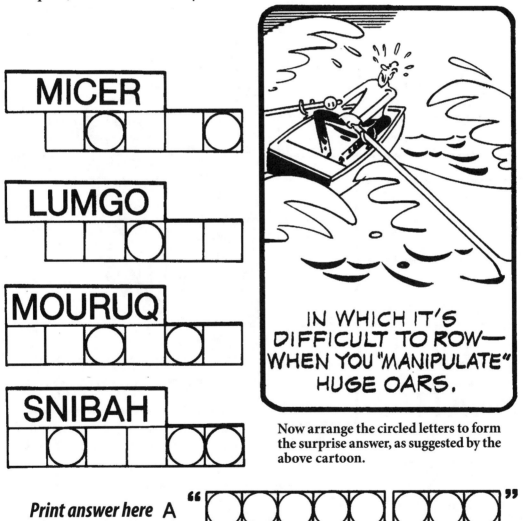

IN WHICH IT'S
DIFFICULT TO ROW—
WHEN YOU "MANIPULATE"
HUGE OARS.

Now arrange the circled letters to form
the surprise answer, as suggested by the
above cartoon.

Print answer here A " ⬡⬡⬡⬡⬡ ⬡⬡⬡ "

JUMBLE®

Unscramble these four Jumbles, one letter
to each square, to form four ordinary words.

ECSEA

PLONY

JOACLE

NATTIC

WHAT THE ALERT
WAITER ALWAYS WAS.

Now arrange the circled letters to form
the surprise answer, as suggested by the
above cartoon.

Print answer here ON HIS " ◯◯◯ " ◯◯◯◯

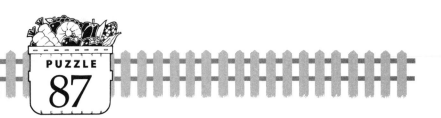

JUMBLE®

Unscramble these four Jumbles, one letter
to each square, to form four ordinary words.

VARGE

DIEFT

DIBOLE

CAMIAN

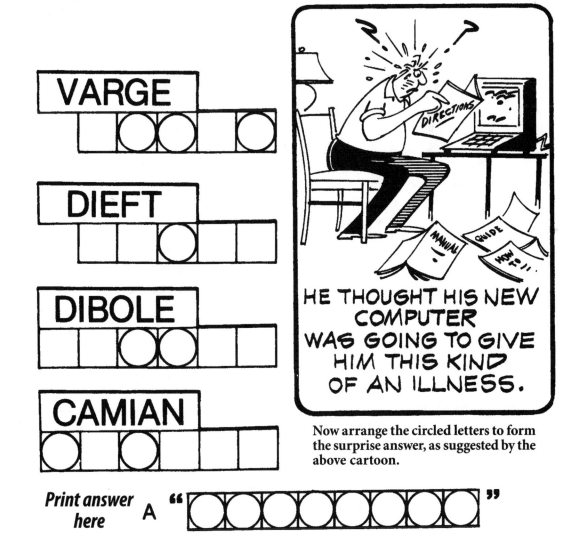

HE THOUGHT HIS NEW
COMPUTER
WAS GOING TO GIVE
HIM THIS KIND
OF AN ILLNESS.

Now arrange the circled letters to form
the surprise answer, as suggested by the
above cartoon.

Print answer
here   A " ◯◯◯◯◯◯◯◯ "

JUMBLE®

Unscramble these four Jumbles, one letter
to each square, to form four ordinary words.

GALOT

SMUCA

CUDINE

SAHDIR

WHAT THAT CRAZY
ARTIST MADE OF
HIS MODEL.

Now arrange the circled letters to form
the surprise answer, as suggested by the
above cartoon.

Print answer here

90

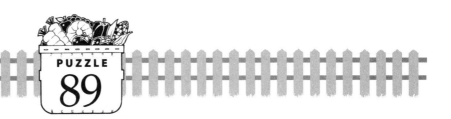

JUMBLE®

Unscramble these four Jumbles, one letter
to each square, to form four ordinary words.

SUYFS

YATTS

SPEEXO

HAREMM

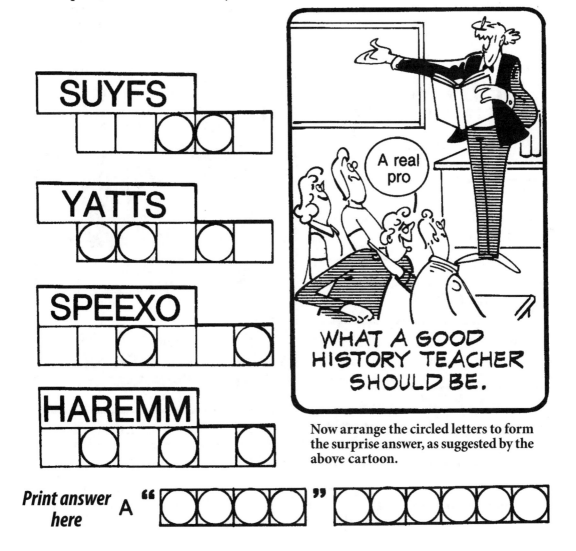

A real
pro

WHAT A GOOD
HISTORY TEACHER
SHOULD BE.

Now arrange the circled letters to form
the surprise answer, as suggested by the
above cartoon.

Print answer here A " ◯◯◯◯ " ◯◯◯◯◯◯◯

JUMBLE®

Unscramble these four Jumbles, one letter to each square, to form four ordinary words.

CREYM

YULST

GREATT

PANNKI

Here's a penny for you, my good man

WHAT A CENT TIP WOULD CERTAINLY MAKE THESE DAYS.

Now arrange the circled letters to form the surprise answer, as suggested by the above cartoon.

Print answer here A " ◯◯◯◯◯◯◯◯ "

JUMBLE®

Unscramble these four Jumbles, one letter
to each square, to form four ordinary words.

CUDEN

SEGUS

MOVULE

ANQUIT

I'm hungry

How much longer?

A WORD OF FIVE
LETTERS THE LAST
FOUR OF WHICH
ARE UNNECESSARY.

Now arrange the circled letters to form
the surprise answer, as suggested by the
above cartoon.

Print answer here " ☐ – ☐☐☐☐ "

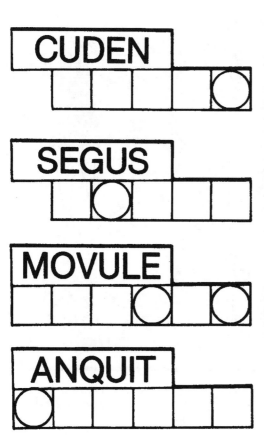

JUMBLE®

Unscramble these four Jumbles, one letter
to each square, to form four ordinary words.

APANG

THONC

BIEFLE

CAFEDE

A girl in every port

THE SAILOR'S MANY
ROMANCES WERE
JUST THIS.

Now arrange the circled letters to form
the surprise answer, as suggested by the
above cartoon.

Print answer here " ☐☐☐☐☐☐ – ☐☐☐ "

JUMBLE®

Unscramble these four Jumbles, one letter
to each square, to form four ordinary words.

GELBI

DEPIT

THENUR

DEFLAB

Should I or
shouldn't I?

WHAT TO DO
WHEN YOU GET THE
FEELING THAT YOU
WANT TO SPLURGE.

Now arrange the circled letters to form
the surprise answer, as suggested by the
above cartoon.

Print
answer
here
◯◯◯ IT IN " ◯◯◯ - ◯◯◯ "
THE

JUMBLE®

Unscramble these four Jumbles, one letter
to each square, to form four ordinary words.

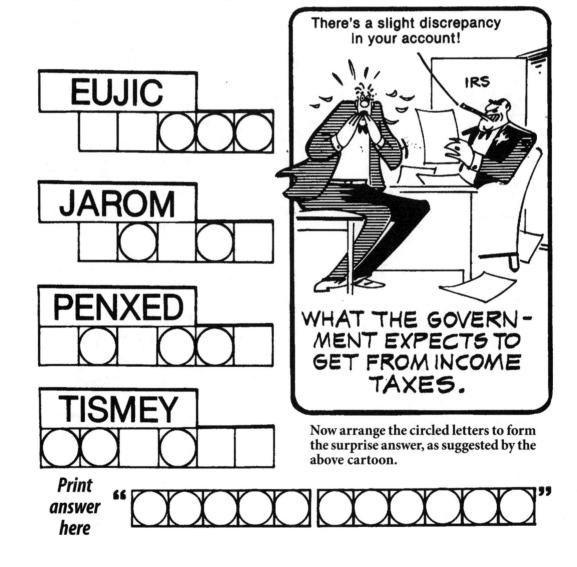

EUJIC

JAROM

PENXED

TISMEY

There's a slight discrepancy
in your account!

IRS

WHAT THE GOVERN-
MENT EXPECTS TO
GET FROM INCOME
TAXES.

Now arrange the circled letters to form
the surprise answer, as suggested by the
above cartoon.

Print
answer
here

" ◯◯◯◯◯◯ ◯◯◯◯◯◯◯ "

JUMBLE®

Unscramble these four Jumbles, one letter to each square, to form four ordinary words.

KALEF

GUAVE

ZOAMAN

GEEREM

LIGHTLY GIVES YOU THE GO-AHEAD.

Now arrange the circled letters to form the surprise answer, as suggested by the above cartoon.

Print answer here

JUMBLE®

Unscramble these four Jumbles, one letter
to each square, to form four ordinary words.

NITLE

INWET

ENFRYZ

ALCIME

He's certainly becoming
well-known

BOOKS

WHAT THE AUTHOR'S
PSEUDONYM WAS.

Now arrange the circled letters to form
the surprise answer, as suggested by the
above cartoon.

**Print answer
here**   HIS "☐☐☐☐☐" ☐☐☐☐

JUMBLE®

Unscramble these four Jumbles, one letter
to each square, to form four ordinary words.

ORFEC

HIDUM

WARTOD

WHEPEN

Not fit for
man nor beast

WHAT A SUDDEN
CLOUDBURST IS.

Now arrange the circled letters to form
the surprise answer, as suggested by the
above cartoon.

Print answer
here   A "⬡⬡⬡⬡⬡" ⬡⬡⬡⬡

JUMBLE®

Unscramble these four Jumbles, one letter
to each square, to form four ordinary words.

ORFUL

LEHEW

TIPEOA

CLAMBE

Can't do a thing with it

WHAT SHE DID
EVERY TIME SHE
WASHED HER
HAIR.

Now arrange the circled letters to form
the surprise answer, as suggested by the
above cartoon.

Print answer here ⬡⬡⬡⬡⬡ HER ⬡⬡⬡

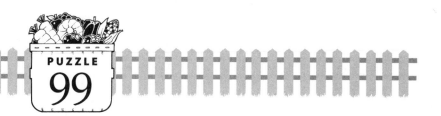

JUMBLE®

Unscramble these four Jumbles, one letter
to each square, to form four ordinary words.

IRYAH

SUROC

MUJERP

DARAMA

There he goes again

WHAT A SLEEP-
WALKER'S HABIT
USUALLY IS.

Now arrange the circled letters to form
the surprise answer, as suggested by the
above cartoon.

Print answer here

JUMBLE®

Unscramble these four Jumbles, one letter
to each square, to form four ordinary words.

CLUHG

SEROU

PATELA

BEGBIT

WHAT BATHING
GIRLS MIGHT BE.

Now arrange the circled letters to form
the surprise answer, as suggested by the
above cartoon.

Print
answer
here

" IN ◯◯◯◯◯◯ ◯◯◯◯ "

JUMBLE®

Unscramble these four Jumbles, one letter
to each square, to form four ordinary words.

YINKK

ZAWLT

LURIAB

ACDAFE

WHAT A QUACK
DOCTOR USUALLY
TRIES TO DO.

Now arrange the circled letters to form
the surprise answer, as suggested by the
above cartoon.

Print answer here ◯◯◯◯ THE ◯◯◯

JUMBLE®

Unscramble these four Jumbles, one letter
to each square, to form four ordinary words.

STEAE

TENFO

COSMAT

NEPELS

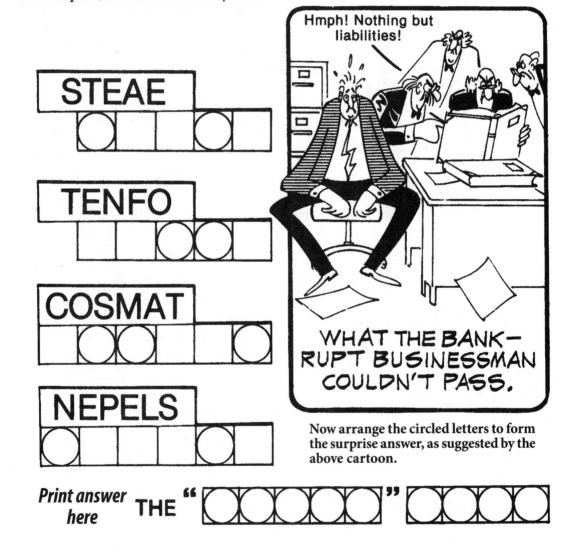

Hmph! Nothing but
liabilities!

WHAT THE BANK-
RUPT BUSINESSMAN
COULDN'T PASS.

Now arrange the circled letters to form
the surprise answer, as suggested by the
above cartoon.

*Print answer
here* THE "⬡⬡⬡⬡⬡" ⬡⬡⬡⬡

JUMBLE®

Unscramble these four Jumbles, one letter
to each square, to form four ordinary words.

TUDAL

GIERT

FLOUBE

REVONG

WHAT SOME
SECRETARIES
HAVE TO TAKE.

Now arrange the circled letters to form
the surprise answer, as suggested by the
above cartoon.

*Print
answer
here* A ☐☐☐ FOR " ☐☐☐☐☐☐☐ "

JUMBLE®

Unscramble these four Jumbles, one letter to each square, to form four ordinary words.

ETIRP

BOYHB

CUSTOC

ORMMEY

HOW YOU HAVE TO LEARN TO TAKE CARE OF A BABY.

Now arrange the circled letters to form the surprise answer, as suggested by the above cartoon.

Print answer here FROM THE ◯◯◯◯◯◯◯ ◯◯

JUMBLE®

Unscramble these four Jumbles, one letter
to each square, to form four ordinary words.

FORVA

SPUHL

FEAMED

BYSUIL

HELD UP IN
BAD WEATHER.

Now arrange the circled letters to form
the surprise answer, as suggested by the
above cartoon.

Print answer here   AN ◯◯◯◯◯◯◯◯

JUMBLE®

Unscramble these four Jumbles, one letter to each square, to form four ordinary words.

SHURC

KNEWA

BOPISH

FITONY

HE'S THE MOST IM—
PORTANT MAN IN THE
RING BECAUSE HE'S
THE ONLY ONE —

Now arrange the circled letters to form the surprise answer, as suggested by the above cartoon.

Print answer here

108

JUMBLE®

Unscramble these four Jumbles, one letter
to each square, to form four ordinary words.

TANGE

HANEY

FRUIPY

REBURB

Gorgeous!

WHAT A FASHION
MODEL MIGHT
FIGURE ON.

Now arrange the circled letters to form
the surprise answer, as suggested by the
above cartoon.

Print answer here

JUMBLE®

Unscramble these four Jumbles, one letter to each square, to form four ordinary words.

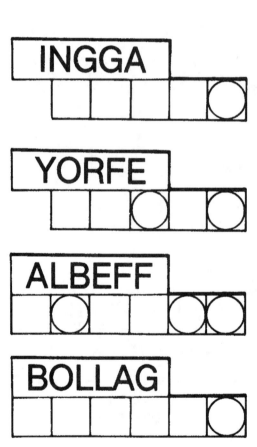

INGGA

YORFE

ALBEFF

BOLLAG

DOES IT ALL COME FROM AN ALLERGY?

Now arrange the circled letters to form the surprise answer, as suggested by the above cartoon.

Print answer here " ⬡⬡⬡⬡⬡⬡⬡ "

JUMBLE®

Unscramble these four Jumbles, one letter
to each square, to form four ordinary words.

DOLOF

SNOWO

LAPLOW

SHINIF

WHAT THAT
PEEPING TOM WAS.

Now arrange the circled letters to form
the surprise answer, as suggested by the
above cartoon.

Print answer here A ⬡⬡⬡⬡⬡⬡⬡ ⬡⬡⬡

JUMBLE®

Unscramble these four Jumbles, one letter
to each square, to form four ordinary words.

DYMAL

ENDOM

NUDEAS

EMBLUF

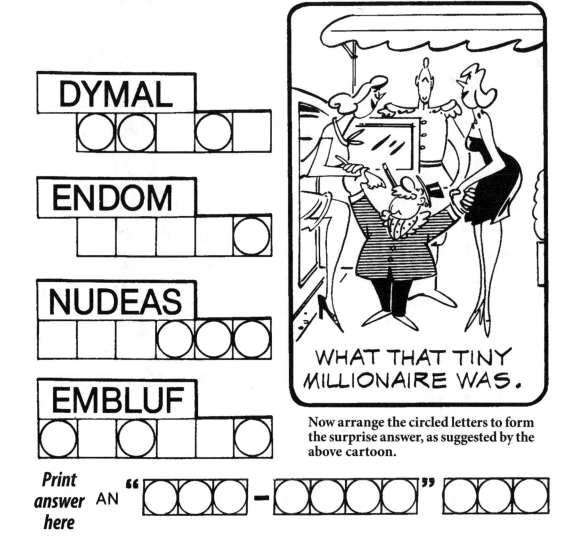

WHAT THAT TINY
MILLIONAIRE WAS.

Now arrange the circled letters to form
the surprise answer, as suggested by the
above cartoon.

*Print
answer
here* AN " ☐☐☐ - ☐☐☐☐☐ " ☐☐☐

JUMBLE®

Unscramble these four Jumbles, one letter
to each square, to form four ordinary words.

OEGOS

YETID

CHINLE

TINVER

Addio

MUCH OF
THE AUDIENCE
AT THAT OPERA
HOUSE WAS THIS.

Now arrange the circled letters to form
the surprise answer, as suggested by the
above cartoon.

Print answer here ◯◯ " ◯◯◯◯◯ "

JUMBLE®

Unscramble these four Jumbles, one letter
to each square, to form four ordinary words.

ROVLE

YOANN

TOOSHE

CUDREE

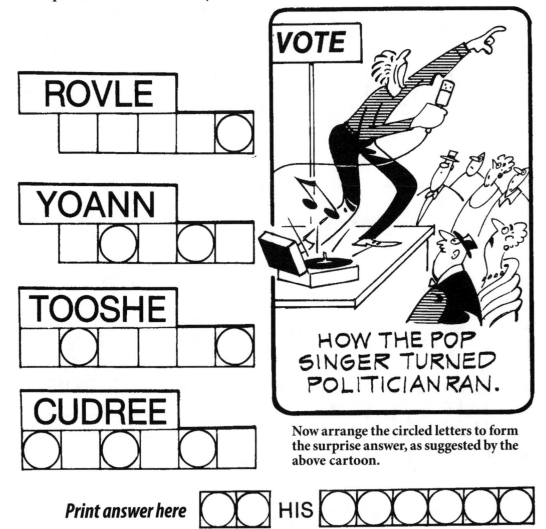

VOTE

HOW THE POP
SINGER TURNED
POLITICIAN RAN.

Now arrange the circled letters to form
the surprise answer, as suggested by the
above cartoon.

Print answer here ⬡⬡ HIS ⬡⬡⬡⬡⬡⬡

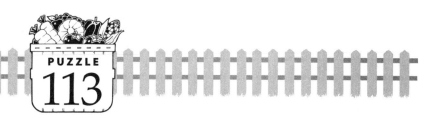

JUMBLE®

Unscramble these four Jumbles, one letter to each square, to form four ordinary words.

RISUV

CLEEX

NOOTIL

ARPITE

Oops!

WHAT AN ALIBI USUALLY IS.

Now arrange the circled letters to form the surprise answer, as suggested by the above cartoon.

Print answer here A " ◯◯◯◯ " ◯◯◯◯◯

JUMBLE®

Unscramble these four Jumbles, one letter
to each square, to form four ordinary words.

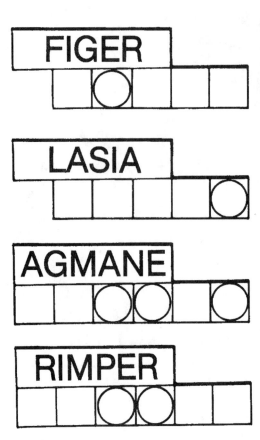

FIGER

LASIA

AGMANE

RIMPER

THE **MARINES**
WERE "ARRANGED"
AS A STUDY GROUP.

Now arrange the circled letters to form
the surprise answer, as suggested by the
above cartoon.

Print answer here " ◯◯◯◯◯◯◯ "

JUMBLE®

Unscramble these four Jumbles, one letter
to each square, to form four ordinary words.

VOLEH

NISOB

CAMEZE

URBBUS

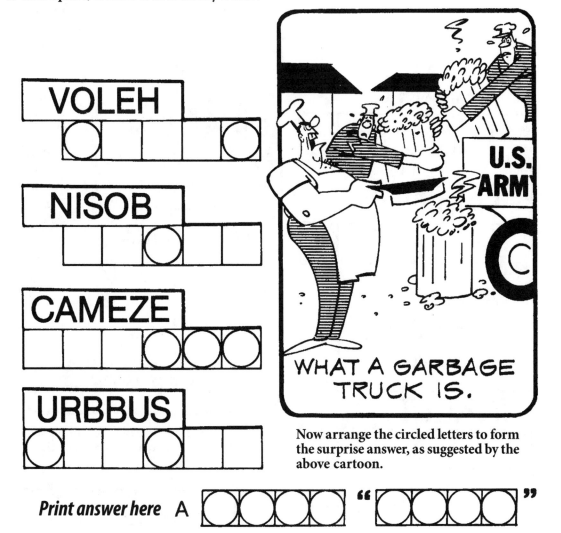

WHAT A GARBAGE
TRUCK IS.

Now arrange the circled letters to form
the surprise answer, as suggested by the
above cartoon.

Print answer here A ⬜⬜⬜⬜ " ⬜⬜⬜⬜ "

JUMBLE®

Unscramble these four Jumbles, one letter
to each square, to form four ordinary words.

YEVAH

TAMID

YURTIP

INKELT

Not a drop of rain in sight

CRACK!

THE ONLY
REALLY RELIABLE
WEATHER "REPORT."

Now arrange the circled letters to form
the surprise answer, as suggested by the
above cartoon.

Print answer here

JUMBLE®

Unscramble these four Jumbles, one letter
to each square, to form four ordinary words.

TAUDI

GEALL

DRUTSY

INSORP

Wait—I've got connections!

WHAT TO DO WHEN
CONFRONTED WITH
A KNOTTY PROBLEM.

Now arrange the circled letters to form
the surprise answer, as suggested by the
above cartoon.

**Print answer
here**

119

JUMBLE®

Unscramble these four Jumbles, one letter
to each square, to form four ordinary words.

MYNEE

DAMMA

TUILGY

DESEEC

THE BEST
LINE TO HOOK
A WOMAN WITH.

Now arrange the circled letters to form
the surprise answer, as suggested by the
above cartoon.

Print answer here " ◯◯◯◯◯ – ◯◯◯◯ "

120

JUMBLE®

Unscramble these four Jumbles, one letter
to each square, to form four ordinary words.

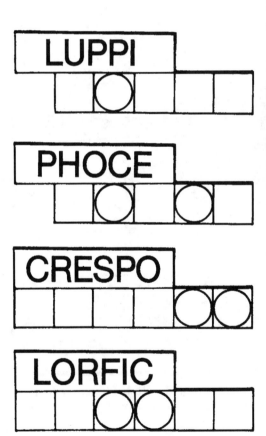

LUPPI

PHOCE

CRESPO

LORFIC

P.D.

THEY MIGHT BE
UP CLOSE.

Now arrange the circled letters to form
the surprise answer, as suggested by the
above cartoon.

Print answer here "◯◯◯◯◯◯◯"

121

JUMBLE®

Unscramble these four Jumbles, one letter
to each square, to form four ordinary words.

NICCY

TAREF

DOAZIC

REMMEB

CONVENIENCE
DINNERS

$ ₹

WHAT THE PRICES
OF SOME OF
THOSE FROZEN FOODS
DEFINITELY WEREN'T.

Now arrange the circled letters to form
the surprise answer, as suggested by the
above cartoon.

Print answer here " ◯◯◯◯◯◯ "

JUMBLE®

Unscramble these four Jumbles, one letter to each square, to form four ordinary words.

CEKOH

GURPE

RANCLE

MUBHEL

Have you decided yet where we're going?

SOMETHING A WOMAN FINDS EASIER TO DO WITH HER FACE THAN WITH HER MIND.

Now arrange the circled letters to form the surprise answer, as suggested by the above cartoon.

Print answer here

JUMBLE.

Unscramble these four Jumbles, one letter to each square, to form four ordinary words.

AGGYB

NISHY

LIFTLE

YEKTUR

THE BIGGEST
PART OF THE FISH.

Now arrange the circled letters to form the surprise answer, as suggested by the above cartoon.

Print answer here ◯◯◯ " ◯◯◯◯ "

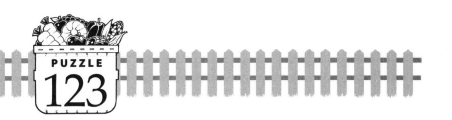

PUZZLE
123

JUMBLE®

Unscramble these four Jumbles, one letter
to each square, to form four ordinary words.

INNEL

LAAVI

BILDOY

HALLET

WHAT A MALE
MOUNTAIN GOAT IS.

Now arrange the circled letters to form
the surprise answer, as suggested by the
above cartoon.

Print answer here A ◯◯◯◯ " ◯◯◯◯◯ "

125

JUMBLE®

Unscramble these four Jumbles, one letter to each square, to form four ordinary words.

You'll have to shape up

WHEN HE TOOK THAT COURSE IN MARINE BIOLOGY HIS GRADES WERE THIS.

VUCER

NOFEL

LAFBLE

CALPEA

Now arrange the circled letters to form the surprise answer, as suggested by the above cartoon.

Print answer here   BELOW   " ☐ " ☐☐☐☐☐

JUMBLE®

Unscramble these four Jumbles, one letter
to each square, to form four ordinary words.

HACTY

TOSOP

AMRUTE

COPILY

Must have
taken lots
of working
out

FROM ATHLETICS
ONE COULD
ACHIEVE THIS.

Now arrange the circled letters to form
the surprise answer, as suggested by the
above cartoon.

Print answer here " ◯◯◯◯◯ ◯◯◯◯ "

JUMBLE®

Unscramble these four Jumbles, one letter
to each square, to form four ordinary words.

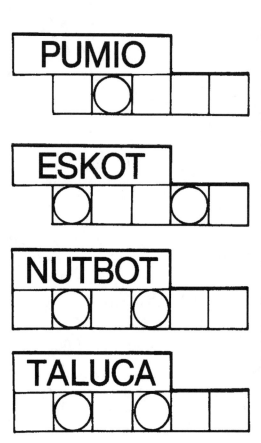

PUMIO

ESKOT

NUTBOT

TALUCA

They say she's a snob

WHAT PINUP GIRLS
SOMETIMES ARE.

Now arrange the circled letters to form
the surprise answer, as suggested by the
above cartoon.

Print answer here

JUMBLE®

Unscramble these four Jumbles, one letter to each square, to form four ordinary words.

SHWIK

DARAW

SYPEDE

NEEGIN

WHAT THE CHURCH SEXTON MINDS.

Now arrange the circled letters to form the surprise answer, as suggested by the above cartoon.

Print answer here HIS ⬡⬡⬡⬡ & ⬡⬡⬡⬡

JUMBLE.

Unscramble these four Jumbles, one letter
to each square, to form four ordinary words.

RUFIT

ARBIN

NAUVEE

SLIMAD

WHILE SHE WAS
GETTING A FACEFUL
OF MUD SHE WAS
ALSO GETTING THIS.

Now arrange the circled letters to form
the surprise answer, as suggested by the
above cartoon.

Print
answer
here

AN ⬡⬡⬡⬡⬡⬡ OF "⬡⬡⬡⬡"

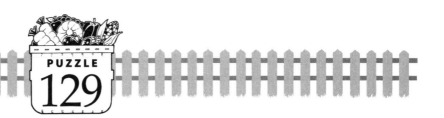
JUMBLE®

Unscramble these four Jumbles, one letter
to each square, to form four ordinary words.

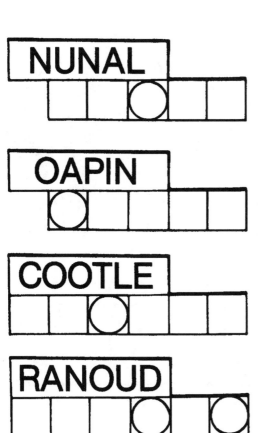

NUNAL

OAPIN

COOTLE

RANOUD

SKIING IS
A SPORT
IN WHICH SOME
END UP THIS WAY.

Now arrange the circled letters to form
the surprise answer, as suggested by the
above cartoon.

Print answer here

JUMBLE®

Unscramble these four Jumbles, one letter to each square, to form four ordinary words.

THOIS

ROGIN

COMIAT

EMSIDE

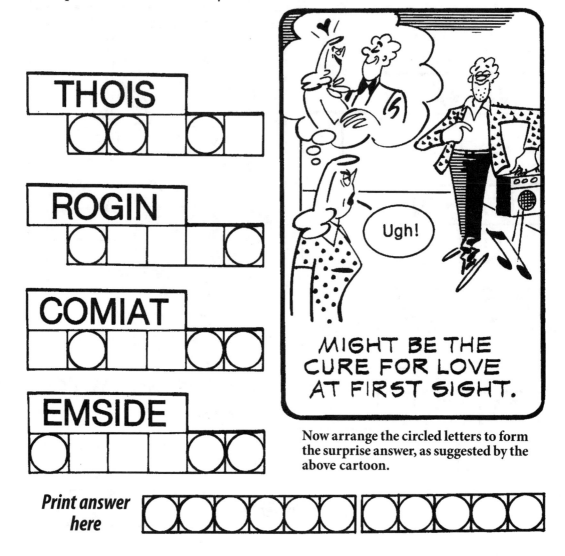

Ugh!

MIGHT BE THE CURE FOR LOVE AT FIRST SIGHT.

Now arrange the circled letters to form the surprise answer, as suggested by the above cartoon.

Print answer here

JUMBLE®

Unscramble these four Jumbles, one letter
to each square, to form four ordinary words.

UGSIE

SAYES

MEENAC

SCEXIE

To our beloved boss!

WHAT SOME
PEOPLE ENJOY
DRINKING TO.

Now arrange the circled letters to form
the surprise answer, as suggested by the
above cartoon.

Print answer here

JUMBLE®

Unscramble these four Jumbles, one letter
to each square, to form four ordinary words.

RELIN

HATIF

NAPHOR

TALKEN

WHAT A SNOWBALL
MIGHT BE.

Now arrange the circled letters to form
the surprise answer, as suggested by the
above cartoon.

Print answer here A "⬡⬡⬡⬡⬡" ⬡⬡⬡⬡⬡⬡⬡

JUMBLE®

Unscramble these four Jumbles, one letter to each square, to form four ordinary words.

SUMEA

ALAFT

HOARIM

VURSCY

WHAT LIFE AT THAT SINGLES BAR WAS.

Now arrange the circled letters to form the surprise answer, as suggested by the above cartoon.

Print answer here A "⬡⬡⬡⬡⬡" ⬡⬡⬡⬡⬡

JUMBLE®

Unscramble these four Jumbles, one letter to each square, to form four ordinary words.

FARCT

NOMUT

CRESIB

PHANEP

HOW HE LOOKED WHEN SHE SEEMED APATHETIC.

Now arrange the circled letters to form the surprise answer, as suggested by the above cartoon.

Print answer here

JUMBLE®

Unscramble these four Jumbles, one letter
to each square, to form four ordinary words.

FYLOT

EVIRT

REFTER

GEPLED

Things sure have changed
since I was his age

THE ONLY THING
COMMON TO
THE PAST, PRESENT
AND FUTURE.

Now arrange the circled letters to form
the surprise answer, as suggested by the
above cartoon.

Print answer here   THE

137

JUMBLE®

Unscramble these four Jumbles, one letter
to each square, to form four ordinary words.

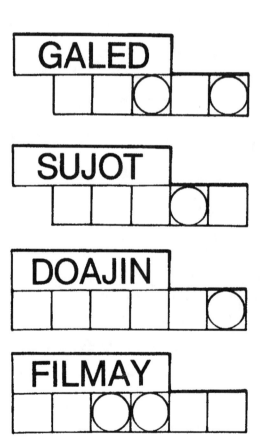

GALED

SUJOT

DOAJIN

FILMAY

WHAT THAT
X-RATED MOVIE
DEFINITELY WAS.

Now arrange the circled letters to form
the surprise answer, as suggested by the
above cartoon.

Print answer here A " ☐☐☐ – ☐☐☐ "

JUMBLE®

Unscramble these four Jumbles, one letter
to each square, to form four ordinary words.

SOULE

PRUNS

TERRAY

DAYDEL

PEOPLE WHO ALWAYS
DO AS THEY PLEASE
ARE NOT LIKELY
TO DO THIS.

Now arrange the circled letters to form
the surprise answer, as suggested by the
above cartoon.

Print answer here

JUMBLE®

Unscramble these four Jumbles, one letter
to each square, to form four ordinary words.

RYBUL

SUMOE

VISPLE

HIWALE

WHAT THAT
INQUISITIVE
CHILD WAS.

Now arrange the circled letters to form
the surprise answer, as suggested by the
above cartoon.

Print answer
here A ⟨○○○○⟩ " ⟨○○○○○⟩ "

140

JUMBLE®

Unscramble these four Jumbles, one letter
to each square, to form four ordinary words.

HALCK

PEWID

OBNIBB

YORRAM

THE MODEL DECIDED
TO MARRY THE
ARTIST BECAUSE
SHE WAS THIS.

Now arrange the circled letters to form
the surprise answer, as suggested by the
above cartoon.

Print answer here ⬡⬡⬡⬡⬡ TO ⬡⬡⬡

JUMBLE®

Unscramble these four Jumbles, one letter to each square, to form four ordinary words.

KRAME
☐☐⬤☐☐

DUFIL
☐☐☐⬤☐

SLYGUN
⬤⬤☐⬤☐☐

ENBLIM
⬤⬤☐☐☐☐

THE FEELING HE GOT WHEN HE SAW THAT THE BOAT HAD SPRUNG A LEAK.

Now arrange the circled letters to form the surprise answer, as suggested by the above cartoon.

Print answer here   A "⬤⬤⬤⬤⬤⬤⬤" ONE

142

JUMBLE®

Unscramble these four Jumbles, one letter
to each square, to form four ordinary words.

TIBOR

WEDIP

RAYWEL

VELCOR

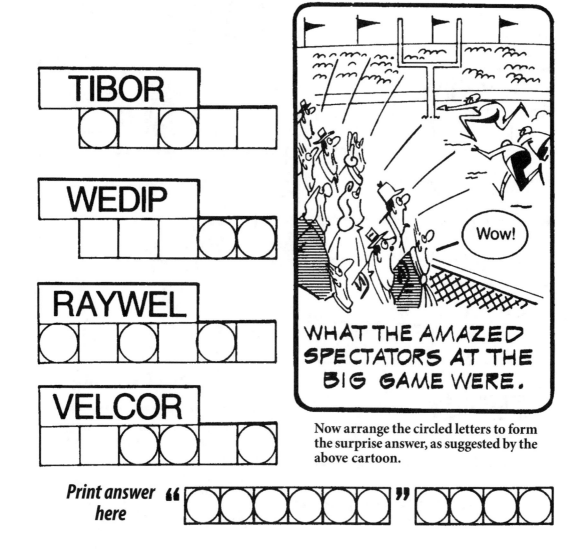

Wow!

WHAT THE AMAZED
SPECTATORS AT THE
BIG GAME WERE.

Now arrange the circled letters to form
the surprise answer, as suggested by the
above cartoon.

Print answer
here
"☐☐☐☐☐☐" ☐☐☐☐

JUMBLE®

Unscramble these four Jumbles, one letter to each square, to form four ordinary words.

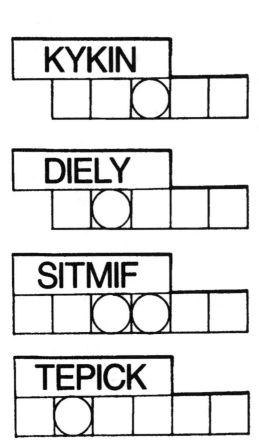

KYKIN

DIELY

SITMIF

TEPICK

WHAT PART OF A FISH IS LIKE THE END OF A MOVIE?

Now arrange the circled letters to form the surprise answer, as suggested by the above cartoon.

Print answer here THE " ◯◯◯ ◯◯ "

JUMBLE®

Unscramble these four Jumbles, one letter to each square, to form four ordinary words.

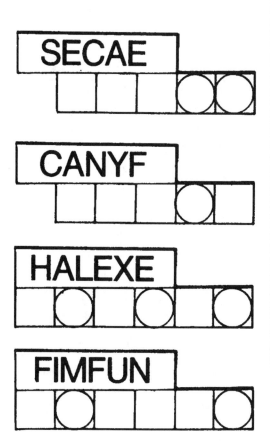

SECAE

CANYF

HALEXE

FIMFUN

Oh, my achin' back

AFTER SHE ASKED HIM TO START WORKING ON THE GARDEN, THE FIRST THING HE DUG UP WAS THIS.

Now arrange the circled letters to form the surprise answer, as suggested by the above cartoon.

Print answer here

JUMBLE.

Unscramble these four Jumbles, one letter
to each square, to form four ordinary words.

PAPYL

CYRUR

YUPTED

ANNKIP

WHAT KIND OF
ATTENTION DID THE
CHAIRMAN GET WHEN
HE RAPPED WITH
HIS GAVEL?

Now arrange the circled letters to form
the surprise answer, as suggested by the
above cartoon.

Print answer here

146

JUMBLE®

Unscramble these four Jumbles, one letter
to each square, to form four ordinary words.

GAILE

KRIHE

SHRAID

REELCY

He's still in bed?!

SOME PEOPLE MIGHT
RISE HIGHER IN
LIFE IF THEY'D
DO THIS.

Now arrange the circled letters to form
the surprise answer, as suggested by the
above cartoon.

Print answer
here

JUMBLE®

Unscramble these four Jumbles, one letter to each square, to form four ordinary words.

ADYLL

VOYNE

TALPEA

ECHTIC

Careful, you'll wrinkle my suit

WHAT AN IMPECCABLE CON MAN IS.

Now arrange the circled letters to form the surprise answer, as suggested by the above cartoon.

Print answer here A

JUMBLE®

Unscramble these four Jumbles, one letter to each square, to form four ordinary words.

GOSUB

YITED

BYBURG

CAPMIT

Now arrange the circled letters to form the surprise answer, as suggested by the above cartoon.

Print answer here   A ⬡⬡⬡⬡⬡⬡⬡⬡⬡⬡

149

JUMBLE®

Unscramble these four Jumbles, one letter
to each square, to form four ordinary words.

NILER

MUPIO

TORRCE

HOMFAT

Wish I had his
bank account

SOME PEOPLE
SCRATCH FOR MONEY;
OTHERS DO THIS.

Now arrange the circled letters to form
the surprise answer, as suggested by the
above cartoon.

Print answer here

150

JUMBLE®

Unscramble these four Jumbles, one letter to each square, to form four ordinary words.

USCOT

AHTEB

SNELET

LAWESE

SHE DATED
ANY MAN WHO
COULD PASS THIS.

Now arrange the circled letters to form the surprise answer, as suggested by the above cartoon.

Print answer here   THE " ◯◯◯◯◯ " ◯◯◯◯

JUMBLE®

Unscramble these four Jumbles, one letter
to each square, to form four ordinary words.

TIFUR

DUIHM

LUMEFF

CLAICO

WHY NO ONE
LAUGHED AT THAT
JOKE ABOUT THE
BROKEN HEATING
SYSTEM.

Now arrange the circled letters to form
the surprise answer, as suggested by the
above cartoon.

Print answer here IT ⬡⬡⬡⬡ THEM ⬡⬡⬡⬡

JUMBLE®

Unscramble these four Jumbles, one letter
to each square, to form four ordinary words.

HIFAT

ORPYX

BALLOG

FUELEY

WHY THE COP
TURNED MUSICIAN
GOT FIRED FROM
THE BAND.

Now arrange the circled letters to form
the surprise answer, as suggested by the
above cartoon.

Print answer here HE WAS "☐☐☐ ☐☐☐☐"

153

JUMBLE®

Unscramble these four Jumbles, one letter to each square, to form four ordinary words.

You're always right, J.P.!

HE OWES HIS SUCCESS NOT TO WHAT HE "KNOWS," BUT TO THIS.

LYMAN

REESA

HOYBIS

WEENST

Now arrange the circled letters to form the surprise answer, as suggested by the above cartoon.

Print answer here

⬡⬡⬡⬡ HE "⬡⬡⬡⬡⬡⬡"

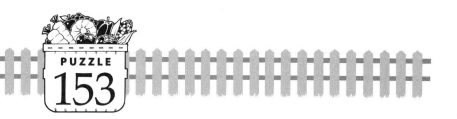

JUMBLE®

Unscramble these four Jumbles, one letter
to each square, to form four ordinary words.

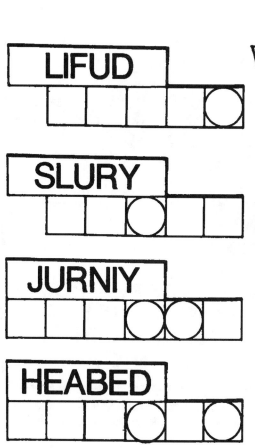

LIFUD

SLURY

JURNIY

HEABED

What a
dirty
job!

But they
interfere
with
navigation

A STERN NECESSITY
ON A BOAT.

Now arrange the circled letters to form
the surprise answer, as suggested by the
above cartoon.

Print answer here A

155

JUMBLE®

Unscramble these four Jumbles, one letter
to each square, to form four ordinary words.

VOARP

ESROU

HARMIO

WHAREK

THE LOAFER PUT
MORE HOURS IN
HIS WORK THAN
THIS.

Now arrange the circled letters to form
the surprise answer, as suggested by the
above cartoon.

*Print answer
here*   ⬡⬡⬡⬡ IN HIS ⬡⬡⬡⬡⬡

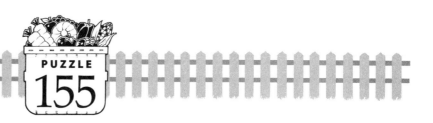

JUMBLE®

Unscramble these four Jumbles, one letter
to each square, to form four ordinary words.

ESING

DYNOW

WHYROT

GYLINK

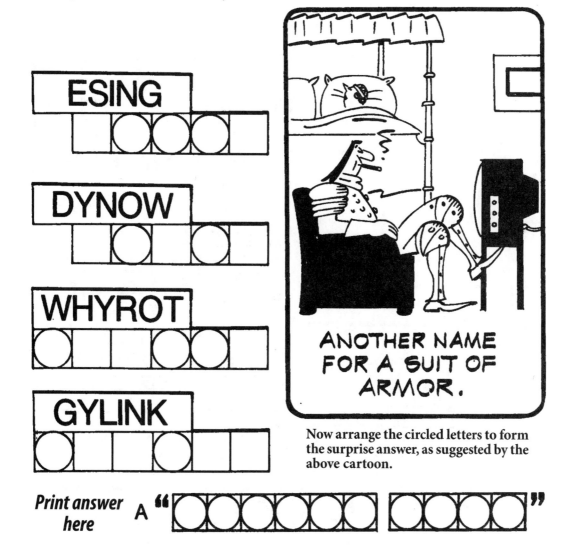

ANOTHER NAME
FOR A SUIT OF
ARMOR.

Now arrange the circled letters to form
the surprise answer, as suggested by the
above cartoon.

**Print answer
here** A "◯◯◯◯◯◯ ◯◯◯◯"

JUMBLE®

Unscramble these four Jumbles, one letter
to each square, to form four ordinary words.

VEVER

TUNDA

YIVELT

BURPES

WHAT THE
ROBOT SURGEON
OPERATED ON.

Now arrange the circled letters to form
the surprise answer, as suggested by the
above cartoon.

Print answer here

JUMBLE®

Unscramble these four Jumbles, one letter to each square, to form four ordinary words.

LIENN

CHOVA

TANQUI

NIRFIM

You may now kiss the bride

WHAT THE JUSTICE OF THE PEACE CHARGED FOR UNITING THEM IN MARRIAGE.

Now arrange the circled letters to form the surprise answer, as suggested by the above cartoon.

Print answer here THE "◯◯◯◯◯◯" ◯◯◯◯

JUMBLE®

Unscramble these four Jumbles, one letter to each square, to form four ordinary words.

PADAT

TARFD

ROBRAW

CYOUTH

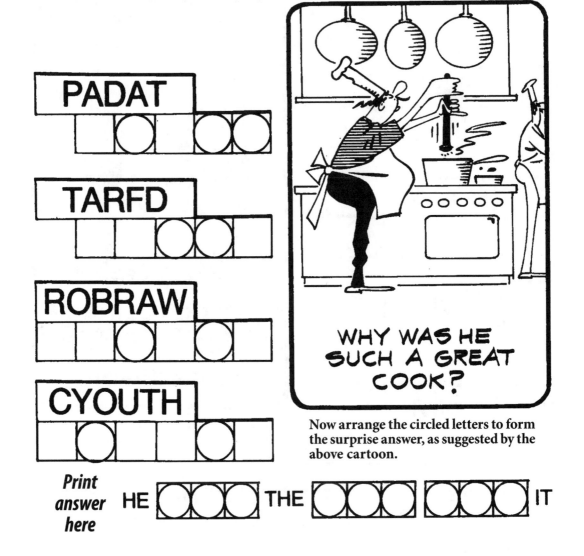

WHY WAS HE SUCH A GREAT COOK?

Now arrange the circled letters to form the surprise answer, as suggested by the above cartoon.

Print answer here   HE ⬡⬡⬡ THE ⬡⬡⬡ ⬡⬡⬡ IT

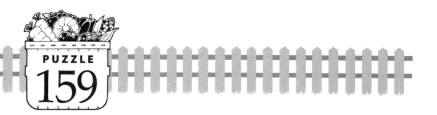

JUMBLE®

Unscramble these four Jumbles, one letter
to each square, to form four ordinary words.

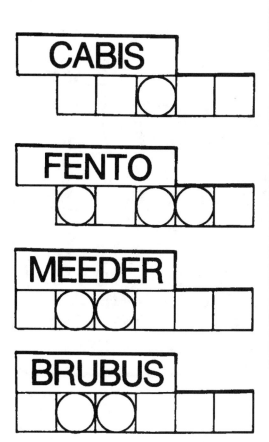

CABIS

FENTO

MEEDER

BRUBUS

Driven by a little old
lady once a month

WHAT MANY A
USED CAR IS NOT.

Now arrange the circled letters to form
the surprise answer, as suggested by the
above cartoon.

Print answer here WHAT IT

JUMBLE®

Unscramble these four Jumbles, one letter to each square, to form four ordinary words.

TIXYS

ROAPE

STYJUL

HIRTHE

WHEN YOU OPEN YOUR MOUTH TO YAWN, IT COULD BE A HINT TO OTHERS TO DO THIS.

Now arrange the circled letters to form the surprise answer, as suggested by the above cartoon.

Print answer here

JUMBLE® Garden

Challenger Puzzles

JUMBLE®

Unscramble these six Jumbles, one letter to each square, to form six ordinary words.

BAGLEM

PLAICH

ELEVAN

CHUNAH

TICILE

RESCIB

STOCK-BROKER

WHAT TO INVEST IN IF YOU DON'T WANT TO GET STUCK.

Now arrange the circled letters to form the surprise answer, as suggested by the above cartoon.

Print answer here

JUMBLE®

Unscramble these six Jumbles, one letter
to each square, to form six ordinary words.

REBOOL

NATTEX

KEPPUE

FERPER

MOAPED

AFDACE

Never stops eating

Runs in her family

WHAT THE NEUROTIC COW HAD.

Now arrange the circled letters to form
the surprise answer, as suggested by the
above cartoon.

Print answer here

A " ☐☐☐☐☐ " ☐☐☐☐☐☐☐

JUMBLE®

Unscramble these six Jumbles, one letter
to each square, to form six ordinary words.

PREFIL

RAWLEY

INTOOM

PRACET

BACHEL

MIRVEN

Happy birthday, Grandpa

Who needs this?

WHAT GRANDPA SAID
HE WOULD DO WHEN
HE WAS GIVEN
A COMB.

Now arrange the circled letters to form
the surprise answer, as suggested by the
above cartoon.

Print answer here

"⬡⬡⬡⬡⬡ ⬡⬡⬡⬡ ⬡⬡⬡⬡ IT"

JUMBLE

Unscramble these six Jumbles, one letter to each square, to form six ordinary words.

GANNIA

TENSOX

VAHBEE

BLAGOM

EXFRIP

ROHTAU

It was all luck— no brains at all

WHEN SUCCESS GOES TO SOMEONE'S HEAD, IT GENERALLY FINDS THIS.

Now arrange the circled letters to form the surprise answer, as suggested by the above cartoon.

Print answer here

167

JUMBLE

Unscramble these six Jumbles, one letter to each square, to form six ordinary words.

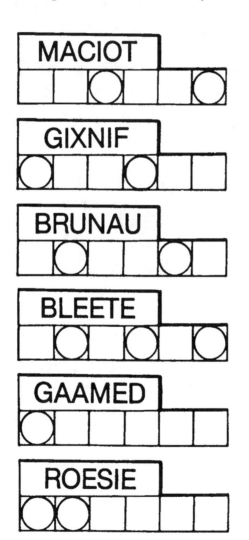

MACIOT

GIXNIF

BRUNAU

BLEETE

GAAMED

ROESIE

WHAT ARE YOU GOING TO DO WHEN YOU GROW UP TO BE A BIG LADY LIKE YOUR MOTHER?

Now arrange the circled letters to form the surprise answer, as suggested by the above cartoon.

Print answer here

" ☐☐☐☐☐ , ☐☐ ☐☐☐☐☐☐☐ "

168

JUMBLE®

Unscramble these six Jumbles, one letter to each square, to form six ordinary words.

WAHELI

HEETES

BINNEG

LAFTOA

STRYVE

ROMMAT

A "*NEW SORT OF MOVE*" BROUGHT FORTH THIS.

Now arrange the circled letters to form the surprise answer, as suggested by the above cartoon.

Print answer here

" ⃝⃝⃝⃝⃝⃝ FOR ⃝⃝⃝⃝⃝ "

JUMBLE®

Unscramble these six Jumbles, one letter
to each square, to form six ordinary words.

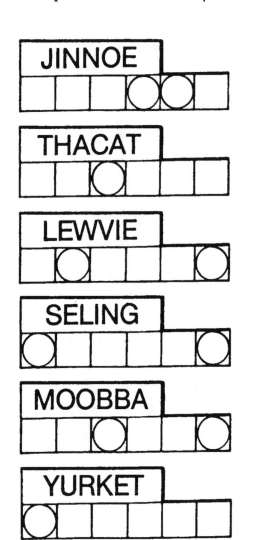

JINNOE

THACAT

LEWVIE

SELING

MOOBBA

YURKET

THEY USED TO
ATTACH WATCHES TO
CHAINS BECAUSE
THEY COULDN'T
AFFORD THIS.

Now arrange the circled letters to form
the surprise answer, as suggested by the
above cartoon.

Print answer here

170

JUMBLE®

Unscramble these six Jumbles, one letter to each square, to form six ordinary words.

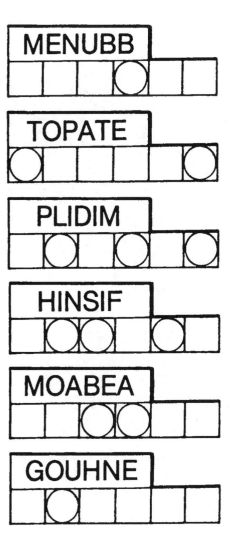

MENUBB

TOPATE

PLIDIM

HINSIF

MOABEA

GOUHNE

WHAT PEOPLE WITH INHIBITIONS SEEM TO BE.

Now arrange the circled letters to form the surprise answer, as suggested by the above cartoon.

Print answer here

171

JUMBLE®

Unscramble these six Jumbles, one letter to each square, to form six ordinary words.

BELTOT

TIXECE

EEFELC

STAUNE

YULTIG

PREEMA

Don't come too near, King Midas

ANYTHING HE TOUCHED TURNED TO GOLD, WHICH IS WHY HE ENDED UP WITH THIS.

Now arrange the circled letters to form the surprise answer, as suggested by the above cartoon.

Print answer here

A " ⬡⬡⬡⬡ " ⬡⬡⬡⬡⬡⬡⬡

JUMBLE®

Unscramble these six Jumbles, one letter to each square, to form six ordinary words.

RETINE

CLINOU

NUHRGY

GLEEBA

ORPAND

TIENIF

THAT OUTLAW WAS CALLED THE STRONGEST MAN IN THE OLD WEST WHEN HE DID THIS.

Now arrange the circled letters to form the surprise answer, as suggested by the above cartoon.

Print answer here

" ⬡⬡⬡⬡ ⬡⬡ " A ⬡⬡⬡⬡⬡

JUMBLE®

Unscramble these six Jumbles, one letter to each square, to form six ordinary words.

CENTED

RIMBAU

SABDUR

TEPICS

BUCHYB

DARAMA

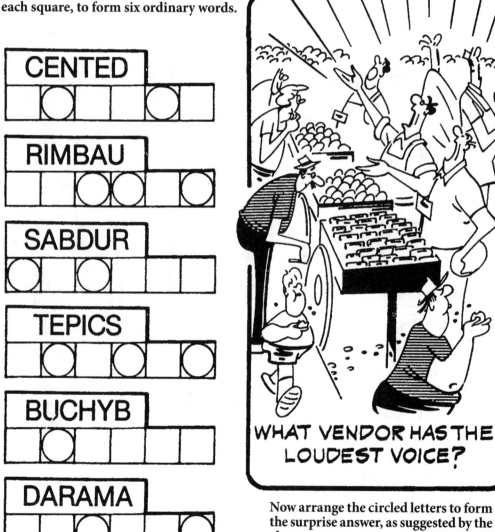

WHAT VENDOR HAS THE LOUDEST VOICE?

Now arrange the circled letters to form the surprise answer, as suggested by the above cartoon.

Print answer here

◯◯◯ " ◯◯◯◯◯◯◯ " ◯◯◯

JUMBLE®

Unscramble these six Jumbles, one letter
to each square, to form six ordinary words.

CASSEC

LUFFIT

DREVIT

HUBILS

PHARME

YURNEP

He's
always
right
down
the
middle

WHAT THE
MUSICIAN TURNED
BALLPLAYER HAD.

Now arrange the circled letters to form
the surprise answer, as suggested by the
above cartoon.

Print answer here

THE ◯◯◯◯◯◯◯ ◯◯◯◯◯

175

JUMBLE®

Unscramble these six Jumbles, one letter to each square, to form six ordinary words.

LEXFAN

CEDBEK

REPIME

INCUVA

SHUBAM

ROHORR

WHAT THAT FASHIONABLE HAIR STYLIST MIGHT PUT.

Now arrange the circled letters to form the surprise answer, as suggested by the above cartoon.

Print answer here

A ⬡⬡⬡⬡⬡ ⬡⬡ YOUR ⬡⬡⬡⬡

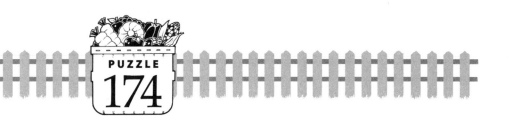

JUMBLE®

Unscramble these six Jumbles, one letter to each square, to form six ordinary words.

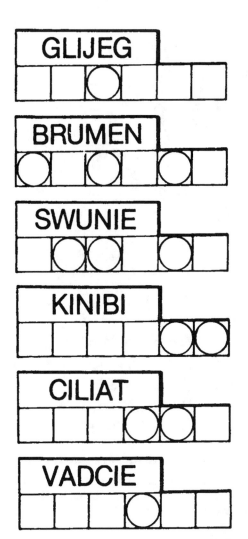

GLIJEG

BRUMEN

SWUNIE

KINIBI

CILIAT

VADCIE

WHAT A GOOD SPORT SHOWS EVEN WHEN HE LOSES.

Now arrange the circled letters to form the surprise answer, as suggested by the above cartoon.

Print answer here

A

JUMBLE®

Unscramble these six Jumbles, one letter
to each square, to form six ordinary words.

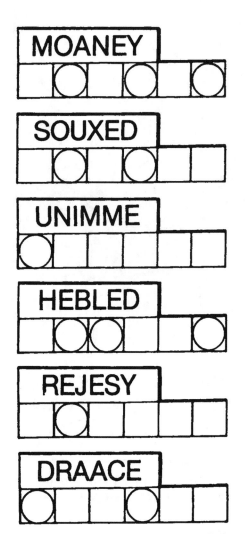

MOANEY

SOUXED

UNIMME

HEBLED

REJESY

DRAACE

A PERSON WHO'S
ALWAYS HITTING THE
CEILING MIGHT
EVENTUALLY HAVE
TO GET THIS.

Now arrange the circled letters to form
the surprise answer, as suggested by the
above cartoon.

Print answer here

HIS ☐☐☐☐ ☐☐☐☐☐☐☐☐☐

JUMBLE.

Unscramble these six Jumbles, one letter
to each square, to form six ordinary words.

PLOARE

REVOOD

CLINAG

WHERDS

SUMPAC

POWNEA

WHAT HAPPENED
WHEN A BUNCH OF
HOODLUMS WENT
SURFING.

Now arrange the circled letters to form
the surprise answer, as suggested by the
above cartoon.

Print answer here

THERE

JUMBLE®

Unscramble these six Jumbles, one letter to each square, to form six ordinary words.

TIPIED

DYRAHL

FIMITS

SULUFE

LUITED

KORBEN

WHAT THEY CALLED THE AMBULANCE'S MASCOT.

Now arrange the circled letters to form the surprise answer, as suggested by the above cartoon.

Print answer here

A ⬡⬡⬡⬡⬡ - ⬡⬡⬡ " ⬡⬡⬡⬡ "

JUMBLE®

Unscramble these six Jumbles, one letter to each square, to form six ordinary words.

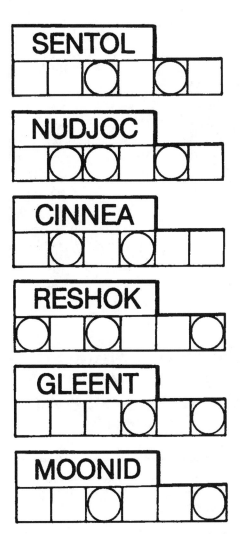

SENTOL

NUDJOC

CINNEA

RESHOK

GLEENT

MOONID

WHAT THE BAKERY TYCOON MUST HAVE BEEN.

Now arrange the circled letters to form the surprise answer, as suggested by the above cartoon.

Print answer here

JUMBLE®

Unscramble these six Jumbles, one letter to each square, to form six ordinary words.

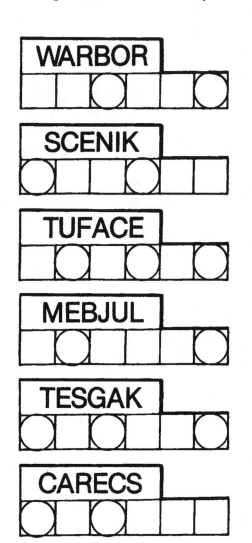

WARBOR

SCENIK

TUFACE

MEBJUL

TESGAK

CARECS

My all-time favorite actress!

WHAT HAPPENED WHEN HE WAS HIT BY A HORSE-DRAWN COACH?

Now arrange the circled letters to form the surprise answer, as suggested by the above cartoon.

Print answer here

HE "   "

JUMBLE®

Unscramble these six Jumbles, one letter to each square, to form six ordinary words.

TELKIN

MAANSE

GRAVEA

FOYFAP

RICCUS

SHIMUL

Harry prefers the waltz

WHAT THE GUY WHO DIDN'T LIKE THE HULA SAID.

Now arrange the circled letters to form the surprise answer, as suggested by the above cartoon.

Print answer here

" ☐☐ ☐☐☐☐☐ ☐☐☐☐☐☐ "

183

Answers

1. **Jumbles:** CRAZE FETID IMMUNE GUILTY
Answer: Could be an expert weight lifter—or dropper—A DIETICIAN

2. **Jumbles:** CRACK ABASH BRAZEN DOUBLE
Answer: What you were the day you first made yourself heard—BORN

3. **Jumbles:** AGLOW PLUME EASILY FAMILY
Answer: On account of this the dramatist was afraid for his life!—"FOUL PLAY"

4. **Jumbles:** HAIRY OWING CLOTHE RAGLAN
Answer: Often produces religious harmony—A CHOIR

5. **Jumbles:** MOCHA BATCH FAMISH HORROR
Answer: Used to "rule the waves."—A COMB

6. **Jumbles:** HONEY GORGE FERRET DISMAY
Answer: The girth could be correct—"RIGHT"

7. **Jumbles:** EMERY CHANT MAROON HARBOR
Answer: What time and grime do—RHYME

8. **Jumbles:** ENVOY TEPID NAPKIN GLANCE
Answer: With this one's required to make a score—NINETEEN

9. **Jumbles:** BELLE HENNA TYPIST POETIC
Answer: What a change of shoe shows—HOSE

10. **Jumbles:** NOISE CHAMP DEMURE ELEVEN
Answer: What the temperamental film star did—MADE A SCENE

11. **Jumbles:** LURID GAVEL ACTING PAGODA
Answer: This horse appears to have some connection with electricity—A PLUG

12. **Jumbles:** PECAN UTTER LEVITY GHETTO
Answer: Once taken you're bound to go under—THE PLUNGE

13. **Jumbles:** KNAVE MADLY ASTHMA REDUCE
Answer: What he was after leaving the tattoo parlor—A MARKED MAN

14. **Jumbles:** FUROR SUMAC EMPIRE INFANT
Answer: Provide the listeners with a cover-up—EARMUFFS

15. **Jumbles:** CABIN PEACE BEFORE MARLIN
Answer: Sounds like headgear for a polar explorer—ICE CAP

16. **Jumbles:** ROBOT ABOUT DEFINE PODIUM
Answer: If you use it your entrance won't leave a bad impression—A DOORMAT

17. **Jumbles:** ABATE FIORD SAFARI POWDER
Answer: Teases with bones—RIBS

18. **Jumbles:** STAID ELATE BAKING TONGUE
Answer: When discharged they disappear—DEBTS

19. **Jumbles:** HOUSE AUDIT CYMBAL PREACH
Answer: Sounds as though you're being pursued when you're just being modest—"CHASTE"

20. **Jumbles:** SWAMP ENACT NICETY HEARSE
Answer: A nodding acquaintance—A YES-MAN

21. **Jumbles:** OFTEN PRIZE THEORY LUNACY
Answer: Only one side was recorded by the artist—A PROFILE

22. **Jumbles:** COUGH EMBER AMBUSH INDICT
Answer: Rescue another way—"SECURE"

23. **Jumbles:** GAILY FRIAR PENCIL CORNER
Answer: How a breadwinner is not apt to spend his time—LOAFING

24. **Jumbles:** RIGOR TOPAZ INTACT BUREAU
Answer: One is supposed to think mechanically—A ROBOT

25. **Jumbles:** AIDED MONEY HINDER VOYAGE
Answer: The good name she lost when she got married—"MAIDEN"

26. **Jumbles:** MOGUL USURP SHANTY JURIST
Answer: It may be this on a golfer when he's in it—"ROUGH"

27. **Jumbles:** MACAW PANSY OPENLY MURMUR
Answer: Inclined to rise to a higher level—A RAMP

28. **Jumbles:** WALTZ POKER AVOWAL DUGOUT
Answer: After treatment, hospital patients are expected to go toward this ward—"OUTWARD"

29. **Jumbles:** SKUNK BOOTY NIBBLE WIDEST
Answer: Headed for winter sports—"SNOW BOUND"

30. **Jumbles:** MURKY TYPED INFIRM GIBLET
Answer: How little devils get together—WITH "IMP-UNITY"

31. **Jumbles:** EAGLE TRYST NUMBER UPSHOT
Answer: What she said when the sculptor arrived—"STA-TUE?"

32. **Jumbles:** IDIOT AORTA FALLEN NEARLY
Answer: "It is NOT spoiled!"—"TAINT"

33. **Jumbles:** PRIME SOUSE CATNIP MOHAIR
Answer: Registered unexpectedly—SURPRISE

34. **Jumbles:** SWOOP QUEST MYRIAD GAINED
Answer: Why a joke caused the carpenter to hurt his thumb—HE MISSED THE POINT

35. **Jumbles:** SMACK LOFTY SHADOW PARISH
Answer: A respectful position on the staff—HALF-MAST

36. **Jumbles:** PARCH DALLY PERSON AVENGE
Answer: A convenient hat for golf—A "HANDY CAP"

37. **Jumbles:** TITLE HURRY SHERRY CROTCH
Answer: "Come here—and beat that girl!"—"HIT-HER"

38. **Jumbles:** LOATH STOKE DONKEY AWHILE
Answer: What you might see at a bar on a rainy night—AN OLD SOAK

39. **Jumbles:** GLOAT AHEAD POTENT EMBRYO
Answer: This wealthy man sounds "attractive"—A MAGNATE

40. **Jumbles:** LOGIC TAKEN BROGUE GYRATE
Answer: Two to one it causes trouble!—A TRIANGLE

41. **Jumbles:** RAVEN LATHE GOLFER PILLAR
Answer: General rearrangement—with greater scope—ENLARGE

42. **Jumbles:** ADAPT VALVE PULPIT MEASLY
Answer: Useful if you go in for spooning in a big way—A LADLE

43. **Jumbles:** BISON MAIZE ADJOIN HELMET
Answer: "Women make ME SAD"—"DAMES"

44. **Jumbles:** AWFUL HUSKY ORATOR NAUGHT
Answer: How to get rid of a tiresome customer—SHOO HIM AWAY

45. **Jumbles:** ELDER TACKY SEETHE BEHAVE
Answer: What the surgeon did after cutting—DEALT

46. **Jumbles:** GLORY SINGE GEYSER BUNION
Answer: What the first letter from his girl left him—IS GIRL

47. **Jumbles:** LOOSE AGONY TINKLE BALLET
Answer: What his "short story" appeared to be—A TALL ONE

48. **Jumbles:** SNOWY GRIEF PRYING JESTER
Answer: You have to give some people the needle to start this—SEWING

49. **Jumbles:** CRUSH PIECE TOUCHY FRENZY
Answer: He got a slap on the face for making it—A PINCH

50. **Jumbles:** SWISH HOARD SAVAGE IODINE
Answer: It generally follows the last course—DISHWASHING

51. **Jumbles:** ALTAR RAINY IMPOSE CLERGY
Answer: Call for a change of letters—ANAGRAMS

52. **Jumbles:** EXERT SNACK GOVERN DINGHY
Answer: This woman's voice sounds penetrating—A SIREN

53. **Jumbles:** RODEO FUSSY INJURY UPROAR
Answer: What he became when he was offered IOU's for an expensive coat—"FUR-IOU-S"

54. **Jumbles:** EXPEL MANGE INLAND FALLOW
Answer: "Come down in the autumn"—"FALL"

55. **Jumbles:** OAKEN ENTRY WEAPON BELONG
Answer: There are many openings in this kind of work—NETWORK

56. **Jumbles:** RAPID SUITE BUSHEL SCENIC
Answer: They do holdups in pairs—SUSPENDERS

57. **Jumbles:** STEED FAINT HERMIT BUSILY
Answer: Starts every month—THE FIRST

58. **Jumbles:** PAPER AISLE FLAUNT CAJOLE
Answer: What you wouldn't expect a fat man to do—"LEAN"

59. **Jumbles:** NOISY DUMPY BEHOLD CANINE
Answer: May be spent in England—POUNDS

60. **Jumbles:** MAGIC ENEMY IMPEDE FIESTA
Answer: He acts dumb—A MIME

61. **Jumbles:** SNACK FLORA JUGGLE PEPTIC
Answer: What he who laughs last often doesn't do—GET THE JOKE

62. **Jumbles:** VYING WAGON MINGLE SNITCH
Answer: What the nearsighted boxer had trouble finding—THE "WEIGH-IN"

63. **Jumbles:** HUMAN POWER DOUBLE WEASEL
Answer: What Eve said when Adam asked whether she still loved him—WHO ELSE?

64. **Jumbles:** EIGHT TRYST EYEFUL MORGUE
Answer: When is the cheapest time to phone your friends by long distance?—WHEN THEY'RE OUT

65. **Jumbles:** PORGY FRIAR HORROR ESTATE
Answer: "Did you hear my last joke?"—"I HOPE SO"

66. **Jumbles:** MEALY BARGE CHARGE TURNIP
Answer: What some bears seem to do in wintertime—"HI-BEAR-NATE"

67. **Jumbles:** MOUTH TACKY DRAGON MYSELF
Answer: The man who stole a pudding was taken into this—"CUSTARDY" (custody)

68. **Jumbles:** PAUSE FRAME EXTENT BOTHER
Answer: What was the trouble with the restaurant they opened up on the moon?—IT HAD NO "ATMOSPHERE"

69. **Jumbles:** FRAUD TAWNY HOURLY LAVISH
Answer: What he said when teacher gave him an "F" on the vocabulary test—WORDS FAIL ME

70. **Jumbles:** RUSTY EJECT MAINLY OPPOSE
Answer: Where you might find the schoolmaster—IN "THE CLASSROOM"

71. **Jumbles:** SORRY BERTH STYLUS GRUBBY
Answer: What the man who was running in short bursts ended up with—BURST SHORTS

72. **Jumbles:** RAVEN NEWLY HECKLE MARMOT
Answer: What four-letter word do some people find most objectionable?—"WORK"

73. **Jumbles:** TRAIT OCCUR RABBIT WEAKEN
Answer: What the successful novelist must have been—ON THE "WRITE" TRACK

74. **Jumbles:** DRAMA BEFOG UNSAID MAGNUM
Answer: From the surgeon came these words—"GO, NURSE!"

75. **Jumbles:** TROTH FOLIO IGUANA TUMULT
Answer: The impression made on one who's been in the Navy might be quite lasting—A TATTOO

76. **Jumbles:** PENCE OCTET HAZING CROUCH
Answer: Fishing maybe a "disease," but it's not necessarily this—"CATCHING"

77. **Jumbles:** DUCHY JULEP PARISH BEMOAN
Answer: Did they call her this because she had a heart of stone?—A PEACH

78. **Jumbles:** BOGUS TOKEN MARLIN YEOMAN
Answer: What much so-called presidential timber often is—MOSTLY "BARK"

79. **Jumbles:** LISLE UNCAP MUSCLE SQUALL
Answer: How that Don Juan treated all women—AS "SEQUELS"

80. **Jumbles:** FINIS HONEY HOOKED BUTANE
Answer: Where the conceited weight lifter let his body go—TO HIS HEAD

81. **Jumbles:** CARGO KHAKI OUTLET MOTION
Answer: What that bakery tycoon was—ONE TOUGH COOKIE

82. **Jumbles:** MANGE SUAVE BEDECK PENURY
Answer: What her appeal sprang from—HER "EYE CUE"

83. **Jumbles:** DRYLY SYNOD ENTAIL BANGLE
Answer: What her ideal became after she married him—AN ORDEAL

84. **Jumbles:** LAPEL OPERA COUSIN PACKET
Answer: What that old-time garage mechanic was bothered with—"CRANK" CALLS

85. **Jumbles:** CRIME MOGUL QUORUM BANISH
Answer: In which it's difficult to row—when you "manipulate" huge oars—A "ROUGH SEA"

86. **Jumbles:** CEASE PYLON CAJOLE INTACT
Answer: What the alert waiter always was—ON HIS "TIP" TOES

87. **Jumbles:** GRAVE FETID BOILED MANIAC
Answer: He thought his new computer was going to give him this kind of an illness—A "TERMINAL" ONE

88. **Jumbles:** GLOAT SUMAC INDUCE RADISH
Answer: What that crazy artist made of his model—A MUDDLE

89. **Jumbles:** FUSSY TASTY EXPOSE HAMMER
Answer: What a good history teacher should be—A "PAST" MASTER

90. **Jumbles:** MERCY LUSTY TARGET NAPKIN
Answer: What a cent tip would certainly make these days—A "PITTANCE"

91. **Jumbles:** DUNCE GUESS VOLUME QUAINT
Answer: A word of five letters the last four of which are unnecessary—"Q-UEUE"

92. **Jumbles:** PAGAN NOTCH BELIEF DEFACE
Answer: The sailor's many romances were just this—"FLEET-ING"

93. **Jumbles:** BILGE TEPID HUNTER FABLED
Answer: What to do when you get the feeling that you want to splurge—NIP IT IN THE "BUD-GET"

94. **Jumbles:** JUICE MAJOR EXPEND STYMIE
Answer: What the government expects to get from income taxes—"EXACT MONIES"

95. **Jumbles:** FLAKE VAGUE AMAZON EMERGE
Answer: Lightly gives you the go-ahead—GREEN

96. **Jumbles:** INLET TWINE FRENZY MALICE
Answer: What the author's pseudonym was—HIS "WRITE" NAME

97. **Jumbles:** FORCE HUMID TOWARD NEPHEW
Answer: What a sudden cloudburst is—A "DROWN" POUR

98. **Jumbles:** FLOUR WHEEL OPIATE BECALM
Answer: What she did every time she washed her hair—
BLEW HER TOP

99. **Jumbles:** HAIRY SCOUR JUMPER ARMADA
Answer: What a sleepwalker's habit usually is—PAJAMAS

100. **Jumbles:** GULCH ROUSE PALATE GIBBET
Answer: What bathing girls might be—"IN SLIGHT GARB"

101. **Jumbles:** KINKY WALTZ BURIAL FACADE
Answer: What a quack doctor usually tries to do—
DUCK THE LAW

102. **Jumbles:** TEASE OFTEN MASCOT SPLEEN
Answer: What the bankrupt businessman couldn't pass—
THE "ASSET" TEST

103. **Jumbles:** ADULT TIGER BEFOUL GOVERN
Answer: What some secretaries have to take—
A LOT FOR "GRUNTED"

104. **Jumbles:** TRIPE HOBBY STUCCO MEMORY
Answer: How you have to learn to take care of a baby—
FROM THE BOTTOM UP

105. **Jumbles:** FAVOR PLUSH DEFAME BUSILY
Answer: Held up in bad weather—AN UMBRELLA

106. **Jumbles:** CRUSH WAKEN BISHOP NOTIFY
Answer: He's the most important man in the ring because he's
the only one—WHO COUNTS

107. **Jumbles:** AGENT HYENA PURIFY RUBBER
Answer: What a fashion model might figure on—HER FIGURE

108. **Jumbles:** AGING FOYER BAFFLE GLOBAL
Answer: "Does it all come from an allergy?"—"LARGELY"

109. **Jumbles:** FLOOD SWOON WALLOP FINISH
Answer: What the peeping Tom was—A WINDOW FAN

110. **Jumbles:** MADLY DEMON SUNDAE FUMBLE
Answer: What that tiny millionaire was—AN "ELF-MADE" MAN

111. **Jumbles:** GOOSE DEITY LICHEN INVERT
Answer: Much of the audience at that opera house was this—
IN "TIERS" (tears)

112. **Jumbles:** LOVER ANNOY SOOTHE REDUCE
Answer: How the pop singer turned politician ran—
ON HIS RECORD

113. **Jumbles:** VIRUS EXCEL LOTION PIRATE
Answer: What an alibi usually is—A "SLIP" COVER

114. **Jumbles:** GRIEF ALIAS MANAGE PRIMER
Answer: The MARINES were "arranged" as a study group—
"SEMINAR"

115. **Jumbles:** HOVEL BISON ECZEMA SUBURB
Answer: Whatw a garbage truck is—A MESS "HAUL"

116. **Jumbles:** HEAVY ADMIT PURITY TINKLE
Answer: The only reliable weather "report"—THUNDER

117. **Jumbles:** AUDIT LEGAL STURDY PRISON
Answer: What to do when confronted with a knotty problem—
PULL STRINGS

118. **Jumbles:** ENEMY MADAM GUILTY SECEDE
Answer: The best line to hook a woman with—"MASCU-LINE"

119. **Jumbles:** PUPIL EPOCH CORPSE FROLIC
Answer: They might be UP CLOSE—"COUPLES"

120. **Jumbles:** CYNIC AFTER ZODIAC MEMBER
Answer: What the prices of some of those frozen foods
definitely weren't—"FROZEN"

121. **Jumbles:** CHOKE PURGE LANCER HUMBLE
Answer: Something a woman finds easier to do with her face
than her mind—MAKE UP

122. **Jumbles:** BAGGY SHINY FILLET TURKEY
Answer: The biggest part of the fish—THE "TALK"

123. **Jumbles:** LINEN AVAIL BODILY LETHAL
Answer: What a male mountain goat is—A HILL "BILLY"

124. **Jumbles:** CURVE FELON BEFALL PALACE
Answer: When he took that course in marine biology his grades
were this—BELOW "C" LEVEL

125. **Jumbles:** YACHT STOOP MATURE POLICY
Answer: From athletics one could achieve this—"LITHE ACTS"

126. **Jumbles:** OPIUM STOKE BUTTON ACTUAL
Answer: What pinup girls sometimes are—STUCK UP

127. **Jumbles:** WHISK AWARD SPEEDY ENGINE
Answer: What the church sexton minds—HIS KEYS & PEWS

128. **Jumbles:** FRUIT BRAIN AVENUE DISMAL
Answer: While she was getting a faceful of mud she was also
getting this—AN EARFUL OF "DIRT"

129. **Jumbles:** ANNUL PIANO OCELOT AROUND
Answer: Skiing is a sport in which some end up this way—
END UP

130. **Jumbles:** HOIST GROIN ATOMIC DEMISE
Answer: Might be the cure for love at first sight—
SECOND SIGHT

131. **Jumbles:** GUISE ESSAY MENACE EXCISE
Answer: What some people enjoy drinking to—EXCESS

132. **Jumbles:** LINER FAITH ORPHAN ANKLET
Answer: What a snowball might be—A " PANE" KILLER

133. **Jumbles:** AMUSE FATAL MOHAIR SCURVY
Answer: What life at that singles bar was—A "MARRY" CHASE

134. **Jumbles:** CRAFT MOUNT SCRIBE HAPPEN
Answer: How he looked when she seemed apathetic—
PATHETIC

135. **Jumbles:** LOFTY RIVET FERRET PLEDGE
Answer: The only thing common to the past present and
future—THE LETTER T

136. **Jumbles:** GLADE JOUST ADJOIN FAMILY
Answer: What the X-rated movie definitely was—A "SIN-EMA"

137. **Jumbles:** LOUSE SPURN ARTERY DEADLY
Answer: People who always do as they please are not likely to
do this—PLEASE

138. **Jumbles:** BURLY MOUSE PELVIS AWHILE
Answer: What the inquisitive child was—A LIVE "WHYER"

139. **Jumbles:** CHALK WIPED BOBBIN ARMORY
Answer: The model decided to marry the artist because she was
this—DRAWN TO HIM

140. **Jumbles:** MAKER FLUID SNUGLY NIMBLE
Answer: The feeling he got when he saw that the boat had
sprung a leak—A "SINKING" ONE

141. **Jumbles:** ORBIT WIPED LAWYER CLOVER
Answer: What the amazed spectators at the big game were—
"BOWLED" OVER

142. **Jumbles:** KINKY YIELD MISFIT PICKET
Answer: What part of a fish is like the end of a movie?—
THE "FIN IS"

143. **Jumbles:** CEASE FANCY EXHALE MUFFIN
Answer: After she asked him to start working on the garden, the
first thing he dug up was this—AN EXCUSE

186

144. **Jumbles:** APPLY CURRY DEPUTY NAPKIN
Answer: What kind of attention did the chairman get when he rapped with his gavel?—RAPT

145. **Jumbles:** AGILE HIKER RADISH CELERY
Answer: Some people might rise higher in life if they'd do this—RISE EARLIER

146. **Jumbles:** DALLY ENVOY PALATE HECTIC
Answer: What an impeccable con man is—A NEAT CHEAT

147. **Jumbles:** BOGUS DEITY GRUBBY IMPACT
Answer: What a wife without curiosity could be—A CURIOSITY

148. **Jumbles:** LINER OPIUM RECTOR FATHOM
Answer: Some people scratch for money; others do this—ITCH FOR IT

149. **Jumbles:** SCOUT BATHE NESTLE WEASEL
Answer: She dated any man who could pass this—THE "ASSET" TEST

150. **Jumbles:** FRUIT HUMID MUFFLE CALICO
Answer: Why no one laughed at that joke about the broken heating system—IT LEFT THEM COLD

151. **Jumbles:** FAITH PROXY GLOBAL EYEFUL
Answer: Why the cop turned musician got fired from the band—HE WAS "OFF BEAT"

152. **Jumbles:** MANLY ERASE BOYISH NEWEST
Answer: He owes his success not to what he "knows" but to this—WHOM HE "YESSES"

153. **Jumbles:** FLUID SURLY INJURY BEHEAD
Answer: A stern necessity on a boat— A RUDDER

154. **Jumbles:** VAPOR ROUSE MOHAIR HAWKER
Answer: The loafer put more hours in his work than this—WORK IN HIS HOURS

155. **Jumbles:** SINGE DOWNY WORTHY KINGLY
Answer: Another name for a suit of armor—A "KNIGHT GOWN"

156. **Jumbles:** VERVE DAUNT LEVITY SUPERB
Answer: What the robot surgeon operated on—BATTERIES

157. **Jumbles:** LINEN HAVOC QUAINT INFIRM
Answer: What the justice of the peace charged for uniting them in marriage—THE "UNION" RATE

158. **Jumbles:** ADAPT DRAFT BARROW TOUCHY
Answer: Why was he such a great cook?—HE HAD THE POT FOR IT

159. **Jumbles:** BASIC OFTEN REDEEM SUBURB
Answer: What many a used car is not—WHAT IT USED TO BE

160. **Jumbles:** SIXTY OPERA JUSTLY HITHER
Answer: When you open your mouth to yawn, it could be a hint to others to do this—SHUT THEIRS

161. **Jumbles:** GAMBLE CALIPH LEAVEN HAUNCH ELICIT SCRIBE
Answer: What to invest in if you don't want to get stuck—A THIMBLE

162. **Jumbles:** BOLERO EXTANT UPKEEP PREFER POMADE FACADE
Answer: What the neurotic cow had—A "FODDER" COMPLEX

163. **Jumbles:** PILFER LAWYER MOTION CARPET BLEACH VERMIN
Answer: What grandpa said he would do when he was given a comb—NEVER PART WITH IT

164. **Jumbles:** ANGINA SECTON BEHAVE GAMBOL PREFIX AUTHOR
Answer: When success goes to someone's head, it generally finds this—NOTHING THERE

165. **Jumbles:** ATOMIC FIXING AUBURN BEETLE DAMAGE SOIREE
Answer: "What are you going to do when you grow up to be a big lady like your mother?"—"DIET, OF COURSE"

166. **Jumbles:** AWHILE SEETHE BENIGN AFLOAT VESTRY MARMOT
Answer: A "NEW SORT OF MOVE" brought forth this—"VOTES FOR WOMEN"

167. **Jumbles:** ENJOIN ATTACH WEEVIL SINGLE BAMBOO TURKEY
Answer: They used to attach watches to chains because they couldn't afford this—TO LOSE TIME

168. **Jumbles:** BENUM TEAPOT LIMPID FINISH AMOEBA ENOUGH
Answer: What people with inhibitions seem to be—TIED UP IN "NOTS"

169. **Jumbles:** BOTTLE EXCITE FLEECE UNSEAT GUILTY AMPERE
Answer: Anything he touched turned to gold, which is why he ended up with this—A "GILT" COMPLEX

170. **Jumbles:** ENTIRE UNCOIL HUNGRY BEAGLE PARDON FINITE
Answer: That outlaw was called the strongest man in the old West when he did this—"HELD UP" A TRAIN

171. **Jumbles:** DECENT BARIUM ABSURD SEPTIC CHUBBY ARMADA
Answer: What vendor has the loudest voice?—THE "I SCREAM" MAN

172. **Jumbles:** ACCESS FITFUL DIVERT BLUISH HAMPER PENURY
Answer: What the musician turned ballplayer had—THE PERFECT PITCH

173. **Jumbles:** FLAXEN BEDECK EMPIRE VICUNA AMBUSH HORROR
Answer: What that fashionable hair stylist might put—A PRICE ON YOUR HEAD

174. **Jumbles:** JIGGLE NUMBER UNWISE BIKINI ITALIC ADVICE
Answer: What a good sport shows even when he loses—A WINNING SMILE

175. **Jumbles:** YEOMAN EXODUS IMMUNE BEHELD JERSEY ARCADE
Answer: A person who's always hitting the ceiling might eventually have to get this—HIS HEAD EXAMINED

176. **Jumbles:** PAROLE OVERDO LACING SHREWD CAMPUS WEAPON
Answer: What happened when a bunch of hoodlums went surfing—THERE WAS A CRIME WAVE

177. **Jumbles:** PITIED HARDLY MISFIT USEFUL DILUTE BROKEN
Answer: What they called the ambulance's mascot—A FIRST-AID "KITTY"

178. **Jumbles:** STOLEN JOCUND CANINE KOSHER GENTLE DOMINO
Answer: What the bakery tycoon must have been—ONE SMART COOKIE

179. **Jumbles:** BARROW SICKEN FAUCET JUMBLE GASKET SCARCE
Answer: What happened when he was hit by a horse-drawn coach?—HE WAS "STAGE STRUCK"

180. **Jumbles:** TINKLE SEAMAN RAVAGE PAYOFF CIRCUS MULISH
Answer: What the guy who didn't like the hula SAID—"NO GREAT SHAKES"

Need More Jumbles?

Jumble® Books

More than 175 puzzles each!

Cowboy Jumble®
$9.95 • ISBN: 978-1-62937-355-3

Jammin' Jumble®
$9.95 • ISBN: 1-57243-844-4

Java Jumble®
$9.95 • ISBN: 978-1-60078-415-6

Jazzy Jumble®
$9.95 • ISBN: 978-1-57243-962-7

Jet Set Jumble®
$9.95 • ISBN: 978-1-60078-353-1

Joyful Jumble®
$9.95 • ISBN: 978-1-60078-079-0

Juke Joint Jumble®
$9.95 • ISBN: 978-1-60078-295-4

Jumble® at Work
$9.95 • ISBN: 1-57243-147-4

Jumble® Ballet
$10.95 • ISBN: 978-1-62937-616-5

Jumble® Birthday
$10.95 • ISBN: 978-1-62937-652-3

Jumble® Celebration
$9.95 • ISBN: 978-1-60078-134-6

Jumble® Circus
$9.95 • ISBN: 978-1-60078-739-3

Jumble® Drag Race
$9.95 • ISBN: 978-1-62937-483-3

Jumble® Explorer
$9.95 • ISBN: 978-1-60078-854-3

Jumble® Explosion
$9.95 • ISBN: 978-1-60078-078-3

Jumble® Fever
$9.95 • ISBN: 1-57243-593-3

Jumble® Fiesta
$9.95 • ISBN: 1-57243-626-3

Jumble® Fun
$9.95 • ISBN: 1-57243-379-5

Jumble® Galaxy
$9.95 • ISBN: 978-1-60078-583-2

Jumble® Garden
$10.95 • ISBN: 978-1-62937-653-0

Jumble® Genius
$9.95 • ISBN: 1-57243-896-7

Jumble® Geography
$10.95 • ISBN: 978-1-62937-615-8

Jumble® Getaway
$9.95 • ISBN: 978-1-60078-547-4

Jumble® Gold
$9.95 • ISBN: 978-1-62937-354-6

Jumble® Grab Bag
$9.95 • ISBN: 1-57243-273-X

Jumble® Gymnastics
$9.95 • ISBN: 978-1-62937-306-5

Jumble® Jackpot
$9.95 • ISBN: 1-57243-897-5

Jumble® Jailbreak
$9.95 • ISBN: 978-1-62937-002-6

Jumble® Jambalaya
$9.95 • ISBN: 978-1-60078-294-7

Jumble® Jamboree
$9.95 • ISBN: 1-57243-696-4

Jumble® Jitterbug
$9.95 • ISBN: 978-1-60078-584-9

Jumble® Journey
$9.95 • ISBN: 978-1-62937-549-6

Jumble® Jubilee
$9.95 • ISBN: 1-57243-231-4

Jumble® Juggernaut
$9.95 • ISBN: 978-1-60078-026-4

Jumble® Junction
$9.95 • ISBN: 1-57243-380-9

Jumble® Jungle
$9.95 • ISBN: 1-57243-961-0

Jumble® Kingdom
$9.95 • ISBN: 978-1-62937-079-8

Jumble® Knockout
$9.95 • ISBN: 978-1-62937-078-1

Jumble® Madness
$9.95 • ISBN: 1-892049-24-4

Jumble® Magic
$9.95 • ISBN: 978-1-60078-795-9

Jumble® Marathon
$9.95 • ISBN: 978-1-62937-548-9

Jumble® Parachute
$9.95 • ISBN: 978-1-60078-944-1

Jumble® Safari
$9.95 • ISBN: 978-1-60078-675-4

Jumble® See & Search
$9.95 • ISBN: 1-57243-549-6

Jumble® See & Search 2
$9.95 • ISBN: 1-57243-734-0

Jumble® Sensation
$9.95 • ISBN: 978-1-60078-548-1

Jumble® Surprise
$9.95 • ISBN: 1-57243-320-5

Jumble® Symphony
$9.95 • ISBN: 978-1-62937-131-3

Jumble® Theater
$9.95 • ISBN: 978-1-62937-484-03

Jumble® University
$9.95 • ISBN: 978-1-62937-001-9

Jumble® Vacation
$9.95 • ISBN: 978-1-60078-796-6

Jumble® Wedding
$9.95 • ISBN: 978-1-62937-307-2

Jumble® Workout
$9.95 • ISBN: 978-1-60078-943-4

Jumpin' Jumble®
$9.95 • ISBN: 978-1-60078-027-1

Lunar Jumble®
$9.95 • ISBN: 978-1-60078-853-6

Monster Jumble®
$9.95 • ISBN: 978-1-62937-213-6

Mystic Jumble®
$9.95 • ISBN: 978-1-62937-130-6

Outer Space Jumble®
$9.95 • ISBN: 978-1-60078-416-3

Rainy Day Jumble®
$9.95 • ISBN: 978-1-60078-352-4

Ready, Set, Jumble®
$9.95 • ISBN: 978-1-60078-133-0

Rock 'n' Roll Jumble®
$9.95 • ISBN: 978-1-60078-674-7

Royal Jumble®
$9.95 • ISBN: 978-1-60078-738-6

Sports Jumble®
$9.95 • ISBN: 1-57243-113-X

Summer Fun Jumble®
$9.95 • ISBN: 1-57243-114-8

Touchdown Jumble®
$9.95 • ISBN: 978-1-62937-212-9

Travel Jumble®
$9.95 • ISBN: 1-57243-198-9

TV Jumble®
$9.95 • ISBN: 1-57243-461-9

Oversize Jumble® Books

More than 500 puzzles each!

Generous Jumble®
$19.95 • ISBN: 1-57243-385-X

Giant Jumble®
$19.95 • ISBN: 1-57243-349-3

Gigantic Jumble®
$19.95 • ISBN: 1-57243-426-0

Jumbo Jumble®
$19.95 • ISBN: 1-57243-314-0

The Very Best of Jumble® BrainBusters
$19.95 • ISBN: 1-57243-845-2

Jumble® Crosswords™

More than 175 puzzles each!

More Jumble® Crosswords™
$9.95 • ISBN: 1-57243-386-8

Jumble® Crosswords™ Jackpot
$9.95 • ISBN: 1-57243-615-8

Jumble® Crosswords™ Jamboree
$9.95 • ISBN: 1-57243-787-1

Jumble® BrainBusters™

More than 175 puzzles each!

Jumble® BrainBusters™
$9.95 • ISBN: 1-892049-28-7

Jumble® BrainBusters™ II
$9.95 • ISBN: 1-57243-424-4

Jumble® BrainBusters™ III
$9.95 • ISBN: 1-57243-463-5

Jumble® BrainBusters™ IV
$9.95 • ISBN: 1-57243-489-9

Jumble® BrainBusters™ 5
$9.95 • ISBN: 1-57243-548-8

Jumble® BrainBusters™ Bonanza
$9.95 • ISBN: 1-57243-616-6

Boggle™ BrainBusters™
$9.95 • ISBN: 1-57243-592-5

Boggle™ BrainBusters™ 2
$9.95 • ISBN: 1-57243-788-X

Jumble® BrainBusters™ Junior
$9.95 • ISBN: 1-892049-29-5

Jumble® BrainBusters™ Junior II
$9.95 • ISBN: 1-57243-425-2

Fun in the Sun with Jumble® BrainBusters™
$9.95 • ISBN: 1-57243-733-2